HOLD *the* ROPE

What others are saying:

"Jeff & Shonn clearly communicate both Biblically and personally how to effectively share the message of God's love and forgiveness."

Dr. Bill Jones, President Columbia International University and Graduate School for Missions Columbia, South Carolina

"Shonn and Jeff have hit a home-run with "Hold the Rope." This book is practical, easy to understand, and easy to implement. This book is a must read for all Christians."

Clay NeSmith, Lead Pastor, Barefoot Church North Myrtle Beach, South Carolina

"Shonn and Jeff have a passion for reaching people for Jesus Christ. This book gives a practical and intentional strategy to help believers share the hope they have in Jesus Christ in everyday life. I highly encourage every believer to read this book."

Robert Lutz, Senior Pastor Shiloh Baptist Church Saraland, Alabama

"There are many people who write books based on information they know, but Jeff and Shonn write this book on truths they live. This is not just information they preach; these are principles they practice day in and day out. You will not only be encouraged to share your faith with others by reading this book, you will also be equipped to share your faith with those you come into contact with every day."

Jared Douglas, President
getalifeministries, Red Oak, Texas

"Jeff and Shonn share a unique insight in witnessing to every culture, social status and age group.

They have continually held the rope for millions of people, preaching the Good News around the globe each year. This book will inspire and motivate all who love God to share His grace and love with others."

Brandon Hensley President,
Team Impact Ministries Dallas, TX

HOLD *the* ROPE

HAVING A HEART FOR THE LOST

JEFF J. NEAL • SHONN KEELS

NEW YORK

HOLD *the* ROPE
HAVING A HEART FOR THE LOST

ISBN 978-1-61448-319-9 paperback
ISBN 978-1-61448-320-5 eBook
Library of Congress Control Number: 2012933818

Morgan James Publishing
The Entrepreneurial Publisher
5 Penn Plaza, 23rd Floor,
New York City, New York 10001
(212) 655-5470 office • (516) 908-4496 fax
www.MorganJamesPublishing.com

Front Cover Design by:
Healey Studios
www.HealeyStudios.com

Interior Design by:
Bonnie Bushman
bonnie@caboodlegraphics.com

In an effort to support local communities, raise awareness and funds, Morgan James Publishing donates a percentage of all book sales for the life of each book to Habitat for Humanity Peninsula and Greater Williamsburg.

Get involved today, visit
www.MorganJamesBuilds.com.

TABLE OF CONTENTS

FOREWORD

As a Senior Pastor, I have held multiple evangelistic outreaches; however, I have not held any events more fruitful than the crusades with Team Impact Ministries. While conducting these crusades, I have had the privilege of becoming friends with two of their lead evangelists, Jeff Neal and Shonn Keels. These men preach the Gospel of Jesus Christ in a way that is both theologically sound and incredibly compelling. Because of their clear Biblical preaching and unquestionable integrity, these men have been asked to preach in some of the greatest churches around the world.

In their book, *Hold the Rope*, they have employed their many years of ministerial experience to provide a wake up call for the Church. In our effort to relate to the world, we have forgotten God has actually called us to go out and reach the lost. In a very straight forward and interesting way, *Hold the Rope* gives us practical and Biblically grounded ways to get others close to Jesus. I pray you will not only read this book; but, you will utilize the methods these men and this book. It is my desire after you read this book you are compelled to hold the rope and get others close to Jesus.

Dr. David Uth
Senior Pastor, First Baptist Church
Orlando, Florida

From Jeff:

This book comes from a passage in Scripture that has become my mandate from God. However, the reason I am capable of fulfilling this call is because of the willing sacrifice of my family. I want to first thank my beautiful wife Cindy, who has allowed me to travel around the world for the last 16 years to share the Good News of Jesus. Words cannot express how much I love you and how thankful I am that God allowed you to be my wife.

I also want to thank my lovely daughter Brooke for her sweet spirit and her gracious input in the editing process. Brooke, your mother and I are blessed to have such a talented daughter. I also want to acknowledge my two sons Dawson and Graham. I love you boys and I know that God has His hand on you to do great things.

Finally, I want to thank the leadership of Team Impact Ministries: Brandon Hensley, Jeff Audas, Keenan Smith, Siolo Tauaefa, and Berry Handley. You men are some of my best friends and I will be eternally grateful that God has collectively called us to hold the rope and get the world close to Jesus.

From Shonn:

Thank you God for the gift of evangelism, and the opportunity to share it with others in print form. Thank you Bonnie, Brelin, and Baylee for supporting and encouraging me along this journey we call life. Your love and support help fuel my passion to make Christ known and to encourage others to do the same.

Thank you Dr. Bill Jones for helping fan into flame God's gift to share Christ with the nations. My time spent with you in seminary changed me for life and has inspired me to tell it often and tell it well.

Thank you Team Impact Ministries for giving me a platform to share Christ with the world.

INTRODUCTION
THE CALL IS CLEAR

There was an older man who lived in a remote village far away from the help of medical professionals. His eyes had been taken over with cataracts, causing him to lose all of his vision. He woke every day to darkness, going about his day with many challenges brought on by his blindness. He often imagined what it would be like to live life outside of the darkness. He longed to be able to see. Each night when he lay to sleep he would pray for his sight to return.

Months passed until a group of missionaries would invade his village with kindness and generosity. Learning of the man's situation, a missionary drove him 100 miles to the nearest mission hospital where a surgery was performed to remove the cataracts from his eyes. The old man who once lived in darkness now saw the light. Although he once was blind, he now could see. His life would forever be changed because of the sacrifice of people like you and me.

The missionaries took the man back to his people and moved on further into the jungle to continue their ministry. After the man returned to his village, he rallied over 50 other people who suffered from the blindness he once knew. He took a long rope and had each one of them hold onto the rope. He then led them 100 miles over the next 22 days to the mission hospital so they could receive the healing he had received. Now that he had seen the light, he did all he could to get his friends out of the darkness so they too could walk in the light.

How much more should you and I who have seen the Light of the world do all we can to lead others to this awesome Light so they may not have to walk in darkness any longer? It would be selfish of us to hoard such an incredible gift. We must give it away. We must tell it often and tell it well so all may know it is possible to walk in the Light. We must do all we can to hold the rope and lead our friends close to Jesus.

When Jesus first walked onto the pages of history to start his earthly ministry, He called men to grab hold of the rope and follow Him. Matthew recorded it this way, "Follow me and I will make you fisher's of men." (Matthew 4:19). Jesus knew where he was leading these men. He told them their destination: Those who follow will fish. If Jesus is leading us to fish, then if we are not fishing, are we really following?

We must answer the call. Jesus not only began His earthly ministry with the call to fish, He closed it with the same call. Just before He ascended into heaven He commissioned His followers to, "Go into all the world and make disciples ..." (Matthew 28:18).

A study of the Greek, the original language of this commission, tells us to make disciples as we are going through life. The verb in this commission is actually "make." The verse could read, "As you go through life, make disciples." Either way, it is clear! Our Lord's first message and His last message to the church were the same. We must do all we can to hold the rope and lead our friends close to Jesus.

When we get to heaven, we will be able to do everything better. We will be able to worship more freely, fellowship more intimately, serve more passionately, and share more faithfully because we will no longer have the flesh to contend with or Satan's influence in this world. However, there is only one thing we won't be able to do in heaven— reach people! When we get to heaven, we will lose our opportunity to hold the rope and get our friends close to Jesus.

Therefore, we must answer the call. We cannot delay. Men and women hang in the balance. The souls of boys and girls are at stake. Our time is short and our work is a matter of heaven and hell. We must get fired up and filled up so we can stand up and speak up for the cause of Christ.

The following pages are designed to encourage and equip you to answer the call with your unique giftedness! God made you special, and He specially made you to reach your world of influence. He has strategically planted you in your network of relationships to reach your friends, family, and associates with the life changing message of the Gospel of Jesus Christ. You can do it!

Please prayerfully read, digest, enjoy and live out the Truth in this book. We are praying for you.

CHAPTER 1

HOLD THE ROPE

There is a treacherous stretch of shoreline off the coast of Africa ominously known as the Skeleton Coast. Without warning, a dense fog can come out of seemingly nowhere. Enormous waves break sharply against jagged rocks that are hidden just below the water's surface. Many ships often crash and sink in the tumultuous waters, taking their crews with them.

Out of compassion for those who were losing their lives in the stormy sea, some residents on the shore formed a lifesaving station. It was a simple endeavor. In fact, there were only four men who volunteered to engage in the original effort.

The men had a tiny shack on the shore where they stored their small lifesaving boat. When they saw the fog come in and the waters become choppy, they would wait on the shore and watch for any ships that might accidentally run up onto the rocks. The men saved hundreds of lives. Their efforts were eventually recognized and chronicled in a feature story in <u>National Geographic Magazine.</u>

After the story ran in the magazine, this lifesaving station became popular. It was so popular that many began to volunteer their time and effort to help in the important work. The one lifesaving boat transformed into five boats overnight. The small shack they had originally built could no longer house the multiple boats. They had to build a larger and much nicer storage building.

After some time, there were literally hundreds of volunteers who spent countless hours at the lifesaving station. One man had an idea that resonated well with all who heard it. This man reasoned since they spent so much time at the lifesaving building they should make it bigger and bring in some comfortable furniture. This first building project turned into another. Eventually, the lifesaving station was the nicest building in town. In fact, it was so nice that they often held weddings and parties in the building. It seemed after a period of time there were more parties than lifesaving efforts.

Finally, on a foggy, cold December night, a massive passenger ship, lost in the darkness, ran upon the jagged rocks. Immediately, the lifesaving boats were deployed, and survivors were being pulled from the deadly waters.

As tremendous effort was being exerted to save lives in the stormy waters, there was a reception taking place in the opulent lifesaving station. During the middle of this reception brave workers began bringing in the survivors of the shipwreck. The people who were at the reception saw the water soaked survivors covered with sand as they tried to enter the station to be treated. Without hesitation, they prohibited them from entering the hallowed halls of this beautiful reception center. The host of the reception explained to the rescuers how the party would be ruined if the filthy survivors were allowed inside. Furthermore, he explained, the carpet would certainly be damaged from the sand and the water, and he simply could not allow this to take place.

After that day, everyone knew what was once a lifesaving station was now nothing more than a social club. The building which was built to save lives was now turning those in need of help away.

In some cases, this story is a sad picture of the church in America today. While I have had the privilege of partnering with some of the greatest soul winning churches in America, I have also observed many churches who are nothing more than social clubs. The church must never forget: She is called to be the lifesaving station.

If you have been a Christian for very long, you certainly have begun to be concerned about the eternal destination of those around you. Often this desire to witness to others is very strong when we first come to the saving knowledge of Jesus Christ. However, as we get overwhelmed with the cares and troubles of our day to day lives, we either suppress or no longer even feel the desire to share the Good News of Jesus.

What would our life look like if every day we were burdened to lead others to Jesus? What if not only did we have the desire to witness to others but indeed we were desperate to see our friends come to know Jesus? Four men in the second chapter of Mark show us what it is to truly be desperate to get our friends close to Jesus. Mark 2:1-12 reads as follows:

> A few days later, when Jesus again entered Capernaum, the people heard that he had come home. So many gathered that there was no room left, not even outside the door, and he preached the word to them. Some men came, bringing to him a paralytic, carried by four of them. Since they could not get him to Jesus because of the crowd, they made an opening in the roof above Jesus and, after digging through it, lowered the mat the paralyzed man was lying on.
>
> When Jesus saw their faith, he said to the paralytic, "Son, your sins are forgiven."
>
> Now some teachers of the law were sitting there, thinking to themselves, "Why does this fellow talk like that? He's blaspheming! Who can forgive sins but God alone?"
>
> Immediately Jesus knew in his spirit that this was what they were thinking in their hearts, and he said to them, "Why are you thinking these things? Which is easier: to say to the paralytic, 'Your sins are forgiven,' or to say, 'Get up, take your mat and

walk'? But that you may know that the Son of Man has authority on earth to forgive sins..."

He said to the paralytic, "I tell you, get up, take your mat and go home."

He got up, took his mat and walked out in full view of them all. This amazed everyone and they praised God, saying, "We have never seen anything like this!"

It is imperative you follow this. These four men have a friend who is not able to walk to Jesus, so his friends bring him to the house where Jesus is staying. The crowd who wants to see Jesus is so dense his four friends could not get the paralyzed man through the front door.

Isn't that ironic? The person who most needed a touch from Jesus could not get to him because of the crowds. Many churches across America do the exact same thing to those "in the world." We push people away from our churches who desperately need a touch from Jesus. Usually, it is not the crowds that inhibit the lost from coming to church. Instead, it is the legalistic regulations.

You know the ones, "If you do not wear a suit and tie, you are not welcome in our church." Or maybe you have heard, "If you are a man and you have long hair you are not welcome at our place of worship." When we impose these man-made regulations, we stop those people from coming to church who most need to be there. In case you are unaware, God has called us to be "fishers of men," not "cleaners of fish."

I want you to notice a difference in these four desperate men. These men were on a mission to get their friend close to Jesus. To what lengths would these four men go? Once they recognized they could not go through the front door, they climbed up on top of the roof. After they got on top of the roof, they cut a hole in the ceiling. They tied ropes onto the mat the paralyzed man was lying on. Then, they held the ropes and lowered the man on the mat through the roof to get him close to Jesus.

Now you have to ask yourself, why would these men exert such great effort to get their friend close to Jesus? These men recognized they could not take him to a doctor who would write a prescription that would ultimately heal him. They also knew a surgeon could not perform an operation that would cause their friend to walk again.

They knew even though they cared for their friend, they had no power, in and of themselves, that would enable their friend to be ambulatory. However, they did have faith. Their faith was this: "If we just hold the rope and get our friend in close enough proximity to Christ, he will be healed."

Perhaps they thought, "We cannot make him better, a prescription cannot make him better, a surgeon cannot make him better. However, if we just hold the rope and get him close enough to Jesus, he will be healed." I strive to live my life holding the rope.

In 1995, after six years of professional football, God called me into full-time evangelism. As a result, I came to God with my resume. I told God I had two things to offer.

Number one, I had above average strength. Number two, I possessed below average intelligence. Seriously though, I could perform feats of strength. People who ordinarily would not attend church came to see these feats of strength. Most importantly, we could then clearly explain the Good News of the Cross of Christ.

Since its inception in 2000, Team Impact has seen well over 300,000 people acknowledge Christ as their Lord and Savior. Of that number, I have not saved even one. I just hold the rope by clearly proclaiming the message of redemption through a relationship with Jesus Christ; I hold the rope and get people close to Jesus. I know if I just hold the rope and get them close enough to Jesus they will be healed. The healing I speak of is not the lame being made to walk, nor is it the blind being made to see. The miracle I speak of is an eternal healing. This healing takes place when someone yields his life to Jesus Christ.

I know I cannot save anyone, but I can show them the way. All members of the body of Christ are called to hold the rope and get others close to Jesus. In what way are you holding the rope and getting others close to Christ? All of us are called to be participants in getting others close to Jesus.

Finally, I want to leave you with one more story. My father is a good man, but he got into his football. Occasionally he would get irritated with the play of our hometown team, the then Houston Oilers. The television knew what he thought of that play, but truthfully it never changed the outcome of a single game. The quarterback never once heard my father's pleas to hit the open receiver on a post route, and the linebacker never heard dad's advice on how to wrap up a tackle. My father was nothing more than an engaged spectator.

Let us never forget, the church is a lifesaving station, not a television. In churches today we need more participants to work in the station, impacting those on the outside looking in, and fewer spectators. Please do not be guilty of being an "engaged spectator." Hold the rope and get people close to Jesus.

CHAPTER 2

HOLD THE ROPE THROUGH RELATIONSHIPS

Relationships are key and fundamental in sharing the gospel. If we desire to influence the world with the gospel, we must build relationships with people who are far from God. Even if we have the Good News of Jesus and we're ready to share, if we have no one to share with, we are useless. Therefore, building relationships will be a key to enabling us to hold the rope and get people close to Jesus. After all, the gospel flows best through the webs of relationships.

John 4:1-38 gives us a 5 step strategy to building relationships with those who are far from God. Read the following verses, and then we will unpack this passage together.

> The Pharisees heard that Jesus was gaining and baptizing more disciples than John, although in fact it was not Jesus who baptized, but his disciples. When the Lord learned of this, he left Judea and went back once more to Galilee.
>
> Now he had to go through Samaria. So he came to a town in Samaria called Sychar, near the plot of ground Jacob had given to his son Joseph. Jacob's well was there, and Jesus, tired as he was from the journey, sat down by the well. It was about the sixth hour.
>
> When a Samaritan woman came to draw water, Jesus said to her, "Will you give me a drink?" (His disciples had gone into the town to buy food.)
>
> The Samaritan woman said to him, "You are a Jew and I am a Samaritan woman. How can you ask me for a drink?" (For Jews do not associate with Samaritans.)
>
> Jesus answered her, "If you knew the gift of God and who it is that asks you for a drink, you would have asked him and he would have given you living water."
>
> "Sir," the woman said, "you have nothing to draw with and the well is deep. Where can you get this living water? Are you greater than our father Jacob, who gave us the well and drank from

it himself, as did also his sons and his flocks and herds?"

Jesus answered, "Everyone who drinks this water will be thirsty again, but whoever drinks the water I give him will never thirst. Indeed, the water I give him will become in him a spring of water welling up to eternal life."

The woman said to him, "Sir, give me this water so that I won't get thirsty and have to keep coming here to draw water."

He told her, "Go, call your husband and come back."

"I have no husband," she replied.

Jesus said to her, "You are right when you say you have no husband. The fact is, you have had five husbands, and the man you now have is not your husband. What you have just said is quite true."

"Sir," the woman said, "I can see that you are a prophet. Our fathers worshiped on this mountain, but you Jews claim that the place where we must worship is in Jerusalem."

Jesus declared, "Believe me, woman, a time is coming when you will worship the Father neither on this mountain nor in Jerusalem. You Samaritans worship what you do not know; we worship what we do know, for salvation is from the Jews. Yet a time is coming and has now come when the true worshipers will worship the Father in spirit and truth, for they are the kind of worshipers the

Father seeks. God is spirit, and his worshipers must worship in spirit and in truth."

The woman said, "I know that Messiah" (called Christ) "is coming. When he comes, he will explain everything to us."

Then Jesus declared, "I who speak to you am he."

Just then his disciples returned and were surprised to find him talking with a woman. But no one asked, "What do you want?" or "Why are you talking with her?"

Then, leaving her water jar, the woman went back to the town and said to the people, "Come, see a man who told me everything I ever did. Could this be the Christ?" They came out of the town and made their way toward him.

Meanwhile his disciples urged him, "Rabbi, eat something."

But he said to them, "I have food to eat that you know nothing about."

Then his disciples said to each other, "Could someone have brought him food?"

"My food," said Jesus, "is to do the will of him who sent me and to finish his work. Do you not say, 'Four months more and then the harvest'? I tell you, open your eyes and look at the fields! They are ripe for harvest. Even now the reaper draws his wages, even now he harvests the crop for eternal life, so that the sower and the reaper may be glad together. Thus the saying 'One sows and another reaps' is true. I sent you to reap what you have not worked for. Others have done the hard work, and you have reaped the benefits of their labor."

Step 1: Strategic Positioning

The first step in holding the rope through relationships is to strategically position oneself around those who are far from God. We must insert ourselves onto the playing field of the unbeliever. We can no longer sit in our comfortable pews and pray for the lost to come to our church. We must go where they are and not expect them to come to us.

In verse 4 of the above passage the Bible says, "Now he had to go through Samaria." Why did he have to go through Samaria?

A study of the first century Jewish culture will quickly reveal a Jew did not normally travel through Samaria when traveling from Judea to Galilee. On the contrary, because the hatred between the Jews and Samaritans was so strong, many of the Jews went eastward traveling from Jerusalem to Galilee, then crossing the Jordan, and passing northward through Perea. This journey on foot typically took about seven days, while the more direct route, through Samaria, typically took only three days. Obviously, Jesus did not practice this tradition of the Jews.

Jesus purposely went through Samaria to strategically position himself into the world of a woman who was far from God. In turn, this divine encounter at the well in Samaria would serve as a launch pad for the message of the

Messiah to be taken into an unreached area. At the well, Jesus held the rope by relating to a woman society had written off as unfit for a friendship.

Jesus did not call us to be a keeper of the aquarium. He called us to be fishers of men. We must strategically enter the world of the lost. After all, this is what Jesus did while here on earth. He pleaded guilty to spending time with crooked tax- collectors, talking with women of ill-reputation, attending raucous weddings and hanging out with the outcasts of society. His motivation was simple: Jesus befriended sinners because they mattered to His Father!

We do not have to look far to position ourselves around those who are far from God. We just need to open our spiritual eyes. We do not have to sign up for a mission trip. After all, as my daughter Brelin once reminded me, "Missions is not just a trip; it is a lifestyle."

Every day as we go about our lives we encounter people who are far from God. We do not have to come up with some new or novel idea of how to personally relate to the lost. We just need to be creative and start right where we are in life. It can be as simple as using one of our hobbies to strategically position ourselves around people who are far from God.

What do you like to do in your leisure time? Do you like to play tennis, golf, basketball, soccer, baseball, etc.? Where do you spend your free time: the library, the gym, the track, etc.? Begin to live like Jesus and spend time in places where there are people who are far from God.

After all, Jesus said, "It is not the healthy who need a doctor, but the sick... For I have not come to call the righteous, but sinners." (Matthew 9:12-12). As you creatively go where lost people are, God will use you to reach people who need him. As you position yourself around lost people, smile often, listen more than you speak, and serve those you are relating to whenever possible. There is a time to be vocal about your faith, but more often, it is a time to listen and be a friend to someone. God will use these practical tools to open doors for you to reach your new friends.

As a senior pastor, I found myself spending all of my time around Christians. I worked at the church all day surrounded by people who loved God. Typically, I would use my lunch hour to spend time with my family, our church staff, our leadership board, or a member of the church. In my spare time, I loved to work out.

In an effort to save time and money, I worked out in my garage with some of the staff guys from the church. Simultaneously, I would regularly challenge the congregation to carry the gospel into their world, but in reality, I realized I was not doing this myself. So, I sold my weightlifting equipment and joined a local gym to strategically position myself around people who were far from God. I trusted God would honor this strategic move and provide me with plenty of opportunities to relate to those who were living apart from Him.

Not long after joining the gym, I started working out with a guy named Patrick. Patrick was a student at the time. He was in very good shape and loved to workout. We would work out together regularly. I never really talked a lot about being a pastor or about the Lord. Mostly, we just talked about working out and what his goals and dreams in life were at the time. Periodically, when it seemed right, I would share pieces of my testimony. Patrick always seemed to listen when I shared. I believe it is because I treated him like a person not a prospect.

I entered his world and became his friend. I never judged him when he shared about his weekend adventures. I just listened and tried to lift more than he did. He always appreciated my competitive spirit.

God would eventually honor our friendship and Patrick would come to visit me in my office at the church. I remember it like it was yesterday. He walked in unexpected but welcomed. He then shared his desire to know the Jesus, which I frequently shared about. He wanted to know the Jesus that had changed my life. I then shared with him a clear presentation of the gospel and invited him to pray to receive Christ as his Lord and Savior. After praying, Patrick asked if he could be baptized on the spot. I rallied our staff together and we baptized him in his street clothes. It was beautiful!

Michael was another guy God brought my way because of our mutual interests. I was volunteering on the local high school football coaching staff and helping out in the weightlifting classes through the school day. Michael was a football coach at the school and also loved to work out. We often worked out together. He noticed the amount of weight I bench pressed and began to ask questions about how he could increase the weight of his bench press. I shared some tips I had learned through the years.

Over the course of time, these conversations grew into more than just working out tips. They grew into conversations about life. Then, Michael started attending our church. Eventually, God allowed me to lead him to Christ, baptize him, and later officiate at his wedding. And to think, this relationship started all because of an interest in being able to lift more weight.

There are people just like Patrick and Michael all over the map. You work with some of them, go to school with others, and live in a neighborhood with many more of them. Look around and get involved in their lives. As you position yourself around these lost people in your circle of influence, God will open up doors for you to build relationships with them. As you know, relationships will prove to be vital in getting people close to Jesus.

Step 2: Strategic Relationships

The second step in holding the rope through relationships is to initiate a growing friendship with those who are far from God.

Once we insert ourselves into the world of the lost we must take the initiative to relate to those who are spiritually bankrupt. Those without Jesus have no hope beyond themselves, and they will not likely ask us how they can find Jesus. We must imitate Jesus and initiate the friendship.

Notice in John 4, as Jesus encountered the Samaritan women at the well, He did not wait on her to ask Him for a drink. Instead, He used their common desire to have their thirst quenched as an opportunity to initiate a conversation with the following question, "Will you give me a drink?" Jesus took the first step and so should we.

A lady from our church once told me of a story that beautifully illustrates this step in holding the rope. Betty worked in a health and wellness environment with a group of young adults. These young adults came to work each week sharing stories of their drunken escapades. Betty never approved of their lifestyles nor did she condemn them for their lifestyles. However, when given permission she spoke freely of how Jesus was the center of her life.

The young adults' respect for Betty grew over time as they worked together in this safe environment. Everyone felt free to be themselves. Once, after a staff Christmas party, one of the young ladies said to Betty, "Thanks for coming to the party. I love how you do not participate in the things we do yet you do not judge us either. You are a great friend."

Betty capitalized on this step of initiating growing relationships with those who are far from God. She was a friend to those who needed a friend the most. She was a shining light in a dark corner of her local community. She never compromised her convictions, yet she never beat her friends over the head with her Bible. She let her life speak, and when given permission, she spoke freely about her faith in Christ. She earned the respect of her friends who were far from God, and the ability to speak hope into their lives on a number of occasions.

This, my friend, is what we are called to do. As I mentioned earlier, the gospel flows best through the webs of relationships.

When I was a student pastor in Flowery Branch, Georgia, there was an incredible group of students who genuinely loved God and wanted to influence their peers with the gospel. This group decided to reach out to a guy named Dan. Dan was a good kid; however, he did not know Jesus. This group really wanted Dan to receive salvation. They decided to reach out to him at lunch every day at school. They went across the cafeteria and invited him to sit with them. They took the initiative to seek him out. They asked him questions about his life, his likes and his dislikes. Dan responded positively to this attention and eventually decided to attend Bible study with them.

After a few months of attending Bible study Dan cornered me on one Wednesday night. He shared with me how he liked what he was learning and how his new friends were unlike any he had ever known. He then shared with me his desire to know Jesus personally.

Because a group of students took the initiative to start a friendship with Dan, I had the privilege of sharing the gospel with him on a Wednesday night and leading him in a prayer to receive Christ as his Lord and Savior.

Jay was a neighbor of mine years ago. He was a former United States Marine. I had served in Desert Storm and Desert Shield as a Navy rescue swimmer, so I thought

I would use the military as a bridge for us to begin a friendship. Periodically, I would spot Jay in the yard and make my way out to engage in a conversation. Many of those early conversations revolved around our former military careers.

However, over time, as life would happen, our conversations would revolve more around work, family, and even spiritual things. Jay went through a tough time and experienced an ugly divorce. God would use this tumultuous time in his life in a very powerful way. Jay would often meet me in the cul-de- sac with many questions. He would ask, and I would do my best to answer. Eventually, these questions would lead to an inquiring of who Jesus really is and what He has done for people like Jay and me.

The moment I prayed for many times became a reality as I shared the gospel with Jay. It was an exciting time as he responded positively to the sharing of the gospel and repented from his past receiving Jesus as both Lord and Savior. Not long after this night, I would have the unbelievable privilege of baptizing him in another neighbor's pool. It was the beginning of a friendship. Jay got plugged into the ministry of our church and has been growing in his relationship with God ever since.

Step 3: Navigating Misunderstandings
This process of holding the rope through relationships will not always be easy. Relationships can be messy, especially when dealing with those who are far from God. You need to prepare yourself for this reality as you are building

friendships with the lost. The third step in holding the rope through relationships is to get ready for misunderstandings.

As sure as death and taxes, misunderstandings will happen among friends. Your new friend who is far from God may not always understand why you want to be his friend. Likewise, your friends in the church may not always understand why you are spending so much time with lost people.

Both of these groups misunderstood Jesus at the well in Samaria. And as sure as the sun rises each morning, there will be times when both of these groups will misunderstand you and me. However, like Jesus, we cannot let these times of misunderstandings frustrate us; rather, we must allow them to fuel our desire to hold the rope and get our friends close to Jesus.

When God drew me into a right relationship with Himself through faith in the Lord Jesus Christ, He called me out of a lifestyle of drugs and alcohol addiction. Not long after having surrendered my life to Christ, I really wanted to influence a friend of mine. Ted wasn't a big drinker, but he did like his beer. One Friday evening Ted asked me to go shoot pool with him at a restaurant. The restaurant also had a bar in it. Although it was no longer my normal practice to hang out in a bar, it was early in the evening, and I felt fairly safe.

Once we arrived, Ted ordered a beer for himself and a coke for me. The server informed me they were out of the cups that were normally used for serving non-alcoholic drinks and asked if I would drink out of the glasses they used to serve mixed drinks. I told her it would be ok. After Ted's three beers and my two cokes, the bar area started filling up, and I started to feel a little uncomfortable. I thanked Ted for the cokes, the pool, and his friendship. Then I headed home.

The next morning I received a phone call from a friend named Victoria. Victoria and I had attended the same high school, and at this time, we also were attending the same church. She was very aware of my former lifestyle of alcohol abuse and also aware of my spiritual transformation. However, when she called me that morning, she immediately accused me of backsliding. Then she asked me what possessed me to go drinking with Ted at the bar. It had only taken about 10 hours for a huge misunderstanding to occur. After I explained myself to Victoria, she encouraged my effort and supported my actions. However, the episode reminded me church people will sometimes misunderstand our desire to relate to and reach people who are far from God.

At the well, the woman did not understand Jesus' genuine interest in her.

"The Samaritan woman said to him, 'You are a Jew and I am a Samaritan woman. How can you ask me for a drink?' (For Jews do not associate with Samaritans.)"

She did not understand why Jesus would risk crossing cultural, gender, racial, and religious barriers to speak with her. His generous spirit did not make sense to her. Others in her past who reached out to her wanted something in return.

This can also happen to you as you desire to build relationships with the lost. As you reach out to the one who is far from God with a "no strings attached" type of love, they may not understand. You cannot let the misunderstanding cause you to lose heart; nor can you give up on the lost. You should expect this misunderstanding and embrace it. It should serve to fuel your desire to hold the rope even more. This misunderstanding does not have to be an obstacle. Instead, it can be an opportunity for you to show the one who is far from God what love really looks like.

As a seasoned believer, Michael desperately wanted his friends to know Christ and regularly reached out to those in his circle of influence. Once he reached out to an extremely wealthy guy, Steven, who was just really getting into the church thing. As their friendship grew, they would periodically do lunch. Michael, not wanting to take advantage of Steven's wealth, made an effort to pay for lunch each time they met.

Eventually this bothered Steven. He told Michael that he was not used to this type of generosity. Most people who took him to lunch expected Steven to pay. Steven simply was not used to someone giving to him with no strings attached. He did not understand how someone could give and expect nothing in return. Get ready for this type of misunderstanding. It will happen. Those who are far from God will not always understand why you want to be their friend. It happened to Michael, it happened to Jesus, and it will happen to you.

The people in our Christian network may not always understand why we are spending time with people who are far from God. After all, even those who were closest to Jesus did not understand why he would reach out to a Samaritan woman.

"Just then his disciples returned and were surprised to find him talking with a woman. But no one asked, "What do you want?" or "Why are you talking with her?"

Did you hear the tone in John's voice, "no one asked?" As the disciples approached the scene at the well, they exchanged their confusion of what was unfolding before their eyes. They did not understand why Jesus would reach out to a Samaritan woman.

If those who were closest to Jesus did not understand his efforts to reach those who were far from God, surely it will happen to us. We must expect it to happen and move forward in spite of the misunderstandings in an effort to hold the rope and get our friends close to Jesus.

Step 4: Love and Acceptance

As you go into the world of the one who is far from God, initiate a growing friendship with your new friend. You must genuinely love and accept people where they are in order to work through the misunderstandings that arise.

Loving and accepting the one who is far from God will serve as the fourth step in holding the rope through relationships.

The greatest need in all the world is to be loved. This need is basic to both Christians and non- Christians. We were all born with this innate desire to be loved. If you are going to hold the rope and get your lost friends close to Jesus, you must love and accept them just the way they are. This pertinent piece of evangelism is where many well intentioned, fully devoted followers of Christ fail. All too often, Mr. Christian takes on the ministry of the Holy Spirit and tries to change his friend. This legalistic approach to evangelism will not work. The ministry of conviction and change is not the Christian's. It is the Holy Spirit's. The ministry of the Christian is to love and accept his friend right where he is. After all, Jesus focused more of His time on connecting with the riffraff of His day than correcting them. Love, not legalism, will move people closer to Jesus. Love should be our single greatest outreach strategy. It is the foundation of the gospel. Love nailed Jesus to the cross, and love draws sinners to Jesus!

I saw this step beautifully illustrated when I was a student pastor of a mega-church just outside of Atlanta, Georgia. One of our leaders in the student ministry was a professional at loving and accepting those others wanted nothing to do with. Rose was married with 4 children and worked full-time as a nurse. However, she was never too busy to volunteer in our middle school ministry. She always connected with students who made some of our church folks nervous. Honestly, some of the students she attracted made me nervous. They often dressed differently, looked differently, and acted differently than the average student who attended church.

One day, I asked Rose how she was going to really reach these students.

She replied, "I am going to love them to Jesus."

She got it! Rose clearly understood the ministry of the church. We are to love our friends and family who are far from God in an effort to get them close to Jesus. Rose did this time and time again as she grew one of the largest Sunday school classes in our ministry.

In my day the question was posed, "What's love got to do with it?" Rose knew that love has everything to do with it.

It is not always easy to love those in your circle of influence who are far from God, but it is always right. As you seek to love those around you, remember you can spell love T-I-M-E.

If you are going to communicate love to those you are building relationships with, you must be prepared to give them your time. As you do life together with those who are far from God, you will be provided with unique opportunities to live out our faith before them in very real and practical ways. You will also be provided with opportunities to love them even when they appear to be unlovable. When you love them, doors will open for Christians to share the message of the gospel. And the gospel is the only message containing the Truth that can set them free from their sin and guarantee them a relationship with God that will last throughout all eternity.

Step 5: Speak

While living and loving is an important part of the process of holding the rope, you must eventually share the message. You cannot fully share the gospel until you open your mouth.

Again, you cannot truly share the gospel until you open your mouth and tell of the Good News of Jesus Christ. If you are to truly hold the rope through relationships, you must eventually take the next and final step: Tell your friend who is far from God about Jesus.

If you are growing in friendship with your lost friend, there will come a time when your friend will be open to what you have to say about Jesus. When this time comes, you must be ready and willing to share with him the greatest story ever told. Jesus left heaven and came to earth by way of a virgin who was supernaturally conceived by the Holy Spirit. He came and lived the life we could never live, a life without sin. Thus, He was worthy to die as a sacrifice for us to save us from an eternal death. God raised Him from the dead to give us eternal life, which we could not earn on our own.

Ultimately, a silent witness is really no witness at all. For the Bible declares, "Faith comes by hearing, hearing the message of Christ." (Romans 10:17).

Paul said, "I am not ashamed of the Gospel, for it is the power of God unto salvation to all who believe..." (Romans 1:16).

People must hear the gospel to believe and be saved, and they will not hear unless we tell it often and tell it well.

Finally, I encourage you to take the initiative to be friendly and observe what is happening among those around you. Choose to be more interested rather than interesting. Make a commitment today to go into your world of influence and initiate growing relationships with those who are far from God. No longer can we expect them to come running to us. We must go to them and seek out their friendships. As we befriend them, we earn the right to be heard.

We all naturally gravitate toward those we already know and trust. People listen to friends. They confide in each other. They let friends influence them. After all, many preachers have taught us, "People don't care how much we know until they know how much we care." Once they know we genuinely care for them, we will be able to share who Jesus is and what He has to offer them.

CHAPTER 3

HOLD THE ROPE
WITH YOUR LIFE

M any years ago, there were two men who were panning for gold in Montana. After just a few days of work, they began to find gold. They did not just find a small amount. Instead, to their delight, they recognized they found a whole lot of gold; more gold than they could collect with the supplies they had. They realized they had to go to town to procure more supplies, so they made an agreement not to tell anyone about the lode they had discovered.

As they made their way into town, they divided up, and without saying a word, they began to purchase the needed supplies. After about two hours, they got on their horses to leave town. They started riding out of their town, but they noticed there were 75 other men on their own horses following them, complete with picks and pans and supplies.

The men quickly exchanged glances. "Did you tell them we found gold?"

"Absolutely not. What about you?" The other quickly asked.

"Of course not."

So one of the men looked at the crowd and asked, "How did you know we found gold, we did not say a word?"

One of the men answered: "Neither one of you had to say a word; your faces showed it all."

We, as born again Christians, have a gift much more precious than gold. If we indeed value the gift, our faces should show it. Our lives should be lived in such a way that purely through example, we hold the rope and get people close to Jesus.

The Bible tells an incredible story of a man who was radically changed by Jesus. In Mark, Chapter 5, there was a man who was possessed by demons. Mark writes:

> "This man lived in the tombs, and no one could bind him any more, not even with a chain. For he had often been chained hand and foot, but he tore the chains apart and broke the irons on his feet. No one was strong enough to subdue him. Night and day among the tombs and in the hills he would cry out and cut himself with stones."

Jesus approached this young man and the demons were sent out to a herd of pigs by a single command of Christ. This man was immediately different. In fact, verse 15 records, "When they came to Jesus, they saw the man who had been possessed by the legion of demons, sitting there, dressed, and in his right mind; and they were afraid." Jesus then commands this young man "to go home to your family and tell them how much the Lord has done for you, and how he has had mercy on you."

I can only imagine this man who had been previously demon possessed walking into his family's home in his right mind. I wonder how his family reacted. I am certain this man would retell the story of how a man named Jesus had freed him. Even if his family did not fully understand what had happened, they could not argue with his transformed life.

Do your friends see you as a different person since you encountered Jesus? I am not asking if you are perfect. But I passionately believe if you have a relationship with Jesus, people should know by the way you act. I want to be clear; I make mistakes every day. However, how I handle those sins says a lot about the fact that I am being sanctified. My lifestyle should daily show I am being changed by the work of the Holy Spirit. This process is called sanctification.

For example, I strive to love my children and to discipline them in a way that ultimately brings glory to God. There have been times when I discipline my children that I raise my voice in a way that is not warranted. Occasionally, I have had to sit my boys down and say, "Daddy made a big mistake; I should not have yelled at you." In these moments my boys are truly touched. They see that I know that I make mistakes and I am willing to take responsibility for those errors.

I hate moving. The only thing I dislike more than moving is helping other people move. Not really, but I like to set the parameters before I even start. Some people are very organized, and it is very easy to help them move. But I've been to other people's homes where the silverware is still in the drawers and they don't even have boxes yet. In cases like that, I normally tell people I will help them move all of the big stuff. So I go to the house, and we move all the couches, the beds, the tables, the chairs, and the dressers. When we are done moving all the big stuff, it looks like we have done a lot of work. In fact, the house looks pretty empty.

The truth is that the real work has not even begun. The real work is the monopoly pieces that fell out of their box in the back of the closest. It's the plates that need to be individually wrapped and packed away. It is these seemingly small, insignificant items one cannot see that take the most time.

Once I got saved, God pretty quickly moved all of the "big sin items" out of my life. On the outside, it looks like I am a decent man. But as God continues to sanctify me, He is still working on the "small items" not apparent to the outside world. I can do the right action with the wrong motive, and it is not pleasing to God. I want to be Holy and righteous – not just on the outside so I can put on a show – but I want my heart to be right. I want the way that I live my life to cause people to question what is different about me. It is then that I will get the opportunity to hold the rope and get them close to Jesus.

Matthew 5:16 says it this way, "In the same way, let your light shine before men, that they may see your good deeds and praise your Father in heaven." Do not deceive yourself, people are watching.

Two of our Team Impact members were on their way home from a crusade, and they had caught a late red eye flight. On the way down to baggage claim, a woman who was working in a bar located in one of the terminals called both of them over. She was busy closing down the bar and emptying a cooler of ice and beer.

"Hey guys, why don't you each take a beer?" She asked.

Both immediately responded, "No thank you."

But the woman persisted, "Seriously guys, they are free. I just want you to have them."

Finally one of the team members responded, "No, thank you anyway. The real reason we don't want one is because we are both Christian ministers, and we do not drink alcohol."

The woman looked back at them with a smile on her face and said, "I know who you are and I know you are Christians. You see, I saw you on TV last night, and I wanted to see if the way you lived matched up with the words you shared last night."

There is a world outside of the four walls of the church that is dying and headed to hell for all of eternity.

This group is begging for authentic Christians. They are looking for people whose lifestyle matches their words. We hold the rope when we model what it is to be a Bible believing Christian. The world recognizes hypocrisy in a moment. At the end of the day, "Christianity is more caught than taught."

We have a member on Team Impact named Siolo Tauaefa. Siolo is a massive individual who was originally born in Western Samoa. He is very strong and can easily bench press over 600 pounds. The only thing larger than his muscles is his sense of humor. Every man on the team recognizes Siolo as the main instigator of almost every practical joke, but the team members are not the only objects of his jokes.

Team Impact is fortunate enough to have men volunteer from local churches that help us when we arrive in a city for a crusade. One service the church provides for us is a driver. This driver will often pick us up from the airport, take us to school assemblies, and bring us to the gym to workout. Obviously, because we spend so much time with these individuals, we develop friendships with them. These drivers are often the perfect target for a Siolo Tauaefa prank.

Here is how the prank goes down. Siolo will often ask one of the drivers to go to the gym to workout with us. Once we enter the gym, Siolo will ask one of the drivers to spot him on the bench press. Usually this request is met with a protest such as, "How am I going to spot you?"

Siolo immediately alleviates their fears and tells them everything is going to be alright. Siolo will gently warm up and before you know it, he will have 500 pounds on the bench press. I have seen Siolo press this weight for repetitions easily. However, Siolo will tell the driver who is spotting him, "I don't know if I can do this or not. Keep your hands on the bar."

The skinny guy spotting him is again really anxious. Next, Siolo lifts the massive weight out of the rack as the victim of the joke holds on to the bar as he was told. The weight then comes all the way down to Siolo's chest before he presses the weight up, ever so slowly. He tells the spotter, "A little help!"

As you can imagine, the volunteer from the church is pulling with all his might but it is having very little effect on the massive weight. Again Siolo will yell, "A little more help!"

This poor guy will use every bit of his strength to try and lift the weight, but Siolo will take this joke to the limit. Often, he will take a full 30 seconds to lift the weight and make the poor guy struggle and pull against the weight.

As the weight is fully locked out, he will look at the spotter and say, "Okay, let's do one more rep."

After both reps are finished, as the volunteer sits down from exhaustion, Siolo will then let him in on the joke. What the spotter failed to recognize is that Siolo had more than enough strength to lift the weight multiple times. In fact, the more he pulled on the weight the less

Siolo pushed. Had the man taken his hand off the bar completely, Siolo would have lifted the weight with ease.

Similarly, we can only live this life in a way that "holds the rope" and get others close to Jesus when we are "filled with the Spirit," letting the Holy Spirit be our strength. As we try to do things under our own power, it will feel as if God is not lifting. In fact, the harder we try "in our flesh," the less God helps. It is only in our weakness that God truly shows up and manifests his power.

God does not need us to spot him. Take your hands off the bar. God's strength is more than sufficient. Jesus told the apostle Paul, "My grace is sufficient for you, for my power is made perfect in weakness." (2 Corinthians 12:9).

In context, Jesus was telling Paul that his physical affliction would not be taken away. Paul then understands what Jesus is saying and responds by saying, "Therefore, I will boast all the more greatly about my weakness, so that Christ's power may rest on me. That is why for Christ's sake I delight in weakness, in insults, in hardships, in persecution, in difficulties. For when I am weak, then I am strong." (2 Corinthians 12:9b-10).

I know a prayer God will answer every time. Will you ask God to help you live your life in such a way it helps draw people close to Jesus? This life be lived through His strength.

Imagine if I were to tell you a department store downtown was offering 56" plasma televisions for $50. People would run each other over in an attempt to purchase one of these bargains. But what if while you were excited about your purchase, you plug in the television, and you find out there is a small catch to your incredible television? The picture does not work. Though it is connected properly, every channel produces nothing more than static. The sound is perfect! Every actor in the movie you are unable to see, because of the defective picture, can be heard clearly.

Eventually, no matter how terrific the sound, you would get frustrated because the television did not produce a picture equal to the audio output. In fact, I bet this television would probably, frustrate you so much that it would eventually end up in the trash.

This society often disregards what we as Christians say because the picture coming through does not match the audio. Our words may be accurate and clear, but our lives are nothing more than static. Saying one thing and living another creates a dissonance the world simply does not understand. I admonish you, live your life in such a way you hold the rope and get others close to Jesus.

CHAPTER 4

HOLD THE ROPE
WITH YOUR
TESTIMONY

I heard a joke about an airplane that was flying over the Atlantic in the middle of the night. Just a couple of hours into the flight, the pilot's voice came over the intercom saying:

"Ladies and gentlemen, this is your captain. We're flying at an altitude of 39,000 feet and at a speed of 568 miles an hour. However, I am afraid I have some good news and some bad news. I will give you the bad news first. We are lost, and we have no idea where we are heading. And now the good news, we are making incredible time!"

This is a great analogy of those without Christ. In the 21st century people seem to be moving at warp speed in their schedules. Between work, school, band practice, girl scouts, dinner club and a host of other events crammed into a weekly schedule, many are busy, and in most cases, their activity represents no significant accomplishments. People are rapidly moving but with very little purpose beyond the here and now. How are these people going to be reached? Who will hold the rope for them? Who will deliver to them the glorious news of the gospel of grace?

I am fully convinced God wants to use people like you and me to carry His message of hope and salvation. However, many are terrified at the thought of sharing the gospel. Many feel they are not qualified to do so, or they simply do not feel they can adequately communicate the Truth.

Perhaps the idea of sharing your faith frightens you as well. Don't let this fear paralyze you. No one can deny what God has done in your life. Your personal story of how God transformed your life through your faith in Jesus Christ is a powerful tool that He can use at any time in your growing relationship with your lost friend. The peace you now experience might be just what your friend needs to hear about. The story of your freedom from your sin may encourage your friend to trust Christ with his whole heart.

You do not have to be a professional to tell your story. Simply work on developing your story into an outline you can comfortably share with your friends. This outline will help you gain the confidence necessary to step out in faith and share your testimony.

The following outline should help serve as a guide for you as you collect your thoughts surrounding your new life in Christ, and the transformation God has started as a result of your salvation experience.

1. Write a paragraph describing your life before Christ.
2. Write a paragraph describing when and why you surrendered to Christ.
3. Write a paragraph describing how Christ has changed your life.

In the rest of this chapter, several testimonies from Team Impact members will be shared as an illustration for you of how to collect your thoughts and put them into a format you can easily share in a conversation with your lost friend. I hope these true stories of lives that have been changed by the transforming power of the resurrected Christ will also motivate you to share your story often.

Cesar Arocha, Jr.

Cesar Arocha grew up in Venezuela in a non-churched home. As an only child, his dad was his hero. However, at age 5, Cesar's dad walked out on his family and headed to the United States of America to chase his selfish dream of becoming a world renowned bodybuilder. After the divorce, Cesar's mother promised to take care of him, and she did a great job until he was about 12 years old. His mother then got involved with drugs and alcohol, and Cesar was sent to live with his grandfather. Shortly after moving in with his grandfather, Cesar found his grandfather dead due to alcohol poisoning. He then went back to live with his mother and started to make bad decisions himself. He felt like his life was spiraling out of control.

At 15 years of age, 10 years after his father left him and went to America, his dad called, pleaded for forgiveness and invited Cesar to come and live with him, his new stepmother and their 7 children. Cesar was angry at his dad but desperately wanted to get to know him, so he packed up and moved to America. His dad and his new family were all Christians. Cesar started going to church for the first time in his life. It was all new to him, but he liked what he was experiencing. On December 31, 2000, after hearing a clear message of how Jesus came from heaven to earth and lived a perfect life, died a sacrificial death, and was raised from the dead for the sins of the world, Cesar confessed his sins to God, put all of his faith in the Lord Jesus Christ, and received the gift of salvation.

Over the last several years, God has been grooming and growing Cesar into a tremendous man of God. His decision making process has changed. He no longer lives for himself. He now lives for his Savior. He graduated from high school as a blue chip all-American in football. He turned down opportunities to play in the ACC and the SEC to play for a small Christian university so he could pursue a degree in Biblical studies. He met and married an incredible young lady who is now the leader of a large middle school ministry in their church. Cesar has been traveling the world with Team Impact since 2006. As good as God has been to Cesar, he regularly confesses the greatest gift God has given him is the gift of eternal life.

Both Cesar and Cesar's dad (also known as Big Cesar) are members of Team Impact. Quite often, on the road, they get to tell their stories together. It is quite an emotional time.

Cesar Arocha, Sr.

Big Cesar was in his early 20's with a dream to be the best bodybuilder on the planet. As Mr. Venezuela and the number one bodybuilder in South America, he left his wife and told his 5 year old son to have a nice life. He then boarded a plane and headed to Atlanta, Georgia to train with Lee Haney – one of the greatest bodybuilders to ever grace the stage. Big Cesar readily admits he was the god of his life. Standing nearly six feet tall and weighing close to 300 pounds, he thrived on the attention of others.

The more people noticed him the better he felt. While training in Atlanta his popularity grew and so did his pride. He believed he had all the answers to life's questions and there was no place for God in his life. However, very soon things would change.

His daily routine of training was interrupted one day when he noticed a beautiful young lady with blonde hair and blue eyes in the gym. She appeared to be everything he was looking for in a new wife. Cesar quickly did all he could to win her attention. Over time he was successful and this young lady, MaryBeth, became his wife. Little did he know, God was going to use her to break his pride and show him his need for Him.

MaryBeth was diagnosed with cancer. This heart wrenching journey would lead them through multiple surgeries with the doctors giving them little or no hope. During this time a friend would begin to share with Cesar who Jesus is. Cesar wanted nothing to do with the Truth his friend shared until one unforgettable night. MaryBeth had just arrived home after some of the most painful procedures in her journey. While she lay in the bed trying to sleep, Cesar realized he had no power to make his wife better. In desperation, he cried out to God for the healing of his wife and the healing of his heart. At MaryBeth's next appointment, the doctor informed them MaryBeth's body was free of cancer. He confessed he did not know how this happened, nor could he medically explain the absence of cancer in her body. Cesar knew then God was real. After returning home, he called his friend and invited him to bring his Bible over and explain to him exactly how he could have a right relationship with God.

Cesar surrendered his life to Jesus and started taking his family to church. As God began to grow him in his new faith, he knew he had some unfinished business. He picked up his telephone and called Venezuela for the first time in 10 years and asked to speak to his son, Cesar. He pleaded for forgiveness and invited him to come to America to live with his new family.

Chip Minton

Chip Minton was living the American dream. He had a beautiful wife, a precious daughter, nice cars, and a big house. He was a two time U.S. Olympian and a WCW wrestler. However, something was still missing in his life. Chip had a huge void that fame and fortune could not fill.

He regularly confesses, "My heart felt like it was wrapped in barbed wire." Alcohol and prescription narcotics soon became his answer to escape the pain and emptiness in his life but to no avail. Eventually he needed more alcohol and moved from prescription narcotics to street drugs trying to fill the deep pit inside his heart. Nothing worked and this destructive pattern eventually cost him everything. He lost his family, his home, his cars, his job, and everything else that mattered to him.

Living in a cheap hotel, drinking and drugging around the clock, trying to mask the pain Chip contemplated taking his life. He planned it out very carefully and fully intended to follow through with his plan; however, God had other plans. Before he could take his own life, the Holy Spirit reminded him of a conversation he had with his mother just days before. His mother is a little Christian woman who is a spiritual giant. She hugged him, told him she loved him, and more importantly, she told him God loved him. God would use the memory of this meeting with his mom to break him.

On his knees, in a dark and dirty hotel room, Chip sincerely cried out to God. For the first time, he confessed his sin and begged for forgiveness. On June 26, 2003, Chip transferred his faith from alcohol to the Almighty and he has never been the same.

Chip has become a different person. His belief in the sinless life, sacrificial death, and resurrection of Jesus has changed him forever. He has rebuilt a friendship with his ex-wife and is actively involved in the life of their daughter. Chip has remained clean and sober and is actively pursuing a degree in Theology. He serves through his local church and enjoys traveling all over the world with Team Impact. However, Chip says the greatest thing about his new life is the hope he has that one day he will live forever in a real place called heaven with God.

Chris McIver

Chris McIver grew up a military brat. Both his mother and father were in the United States Army. Before settling in Texas as a teenager, Chris had lived all over the world and really  was not sure what state or country to refer to as home. Even though the McIver's moved often, Chris' parents made sure he grew up in a church. At this point, Chris considered himself to be a religious person as he practiced the sacraments, and all of the other rituals that were a part of his Sunday routine.

Chris was a good guy growing up. He did not use drugs, drink alcohol or participate in any rebellious activity. However, at 17 years of age at a Fellowship of Christian Athletes event, Chris realized for the first time in his life his need for a Savior. His coaches invited him along with several other athletes to come to a big night of games, food and fun. While at the event, a speaker shared about how all have sinned and fallen short of the glory of God. The speaker explained how sin separated man from God, and if a man dies in his sin, he will spend an eternity in a real place called hell. The speaker went on to tell how Jesus left heaven and came to earth to live a life man could never live, to die a death man deserved, and to pay a price man could never pay. He also told of the resurrection of Jesus and how all who would come to Jesus in child like faith could be forgiven of their sins and have a home in heaven.

Chris wanted this home in heaven. He desired a real relationship with God. On that night, for the first time in his life, Chris sincerely confessed his sins to God and believed with all his heart in the Lord Jesus Christ for his salvation. Chris no longer searches for significance in things, people, accolades, or status. Instead, he has found his identity in Christ. He no longer tries to earn God's love through tradition and rituals. Instead, he has truly accepted God's grace. God has blessed Chris with a beautiful wife, a precious daughter, the ability to travel in ministry with Team Impact, and the opportunity to see many of his dreams come true. However, the greatest thing God has done for Chris is give him the hope of a place he can call home for all of eternity — heaven.

Randall Harris

Randall Harris often uses a story to share his testimony. One night at one of our Team Impact events, Randall was responsible for doing the concrete and ice breaks on fire. Because of the ice melting, the floor was a little slippery. After the fuel had been poured over the breaks another team member lit the fuel, and the stage burst into flames. Randall excitedly jumped around the stage in the midst of the flames, breaking one stack after another while the crowd cheered in excitement.

After breaking several stacks, Randall looked and saw there was one small stack of ice left at the front center of the stage. He then ran and jumped off of a stack of blocks. While flying in the air, he did a scissor kick to break the stack of ice.

Let me interject at this point, Randal is about 5'10" tall and is a very big guy. We do not know exactly how much Randall weighs because he keeps his weight a secret, but it's probably more than 300 pounds – far more than a man should weigh if he is going to jump around in the air like a flying tornado.

When Randall landed, he fell to the ground. He then made three attempts to get up and walk off the stage. With each attempt, Randall would step and then hit the ground. A doctor in the crowd noticed Randall's inability to walk and met him behind the curtain as he crawled off stage. The doctor insisted Randall go to the emergency room to get checked out. While in the emergency room, at first glance, they could find nothing wrong with his leg. On the outside, it looked totally normal. However, an x-ray would prove this was not the case. Randall's leg was shattered in a couple of places. On the outside it looked good, but under the surface, it was a mess. So it was with the story of his life.

Randall grew up in a Christian home. He was taught the Bible from a very early age. His family attended church weekly and was very involved in the ministries of their church. Randall knew all the verses, sang all the songs, knew when to sit, stand, clap, and all of the other things that took place in his church. Randall was an all around good guy. However, deep down, on the inside, there was something missing. Even though he grew up in church, he had not grown up in Christ. And there is a difference.

At the age of 17, God opened Randall's spiritual eyes and showed him his own righteousness was like filthy rags. Randall understood for the first time he needed Jesus. The death, burial, and resurrection of Christ took on a whole new meaning for him. He personalized it and truly transferred his faith from his own righteousness to the One who became sin so Randall could become the righteousness of God.

After believing on the Lord Jesus Christ and receiving salvation, Randall became a new person. This shy, quiet, mammoth of a man who once depended on his own goodness is now a gospel sharing machine who depends solely on grace. God has blessed Randall tremendously. He is married to an incredible Christian lady. He travels full-time with Team Impact. And he is one of the strongest natural powerlifters in the world with many titles and trophies to prove it. However, Randall regularly testifies the greatest gift God has given him is the gift of eternal life. He knows without a shadow of a doubt when he dies, he will spend forever with God in a real place called heaven.

Hunter Grimes

Growing up as a child was very difficult for Hunter Grimes. Physical abuse from his alcoholic father was something he feared each day as a little boy. Hunter once said when sharing his story, "I remember as a child opening the refrigerator door and seeing the brown bag, the same type  of brown bag that was in my dad's hand every time he came home from work." The stuff in the brown bag took over Hunter's dad's life and fueled his anger as he often took it out on Hunter's mother, his sisters, and him. Hunter would often go to sleep to the sounds of his mother's cries as she would often wait up on her drunken husband to return home from a night on the town. Hunter's mom was a faithful woman. Many nights in the midst of her crying, Hunter would hear her crying out in prayer for her husband. She would also pray for her children and raise them in the church.

When Hunter reached high school, things started to change for the good. His father surrendered his life to Jesus Christ and gave up his old way of life. Hunter remembers seeing his dad on the sidelines cheering for him at the football games. At this stage in Hunter's life, he had a renewed relationship with his dad. However, in May of

1993, his father died in a vehicle accident. The accident had a huge impact on Hunter for the next several years. He was the first person on the scene of the accident, and the last person to see his father alive. Hunter would begin to question God and the reality of His existence. He watched his alcoholic father surrender his life to Christ, begin to love and support his family like never before, and then die in a car accident.

Hunter became angry and started living the out of control life his father once lived. With his life spiraling out of control, Hunter lost everything. With nowhere to go and nowhere to turn, Hunter finally looked up. In 1998, he fell to his knees and asked Jesus to forgive him of his sins, take control of his life and give him a brand new start.

The commitment Hunter made to Christ has changed him forever and secured him a home in heaven. Like the change in his father's life, Hunter is a different person, and he is leading his family in the way of the Lord. God has strategically placed him in a strong position of influence as the Chief of Police in Walker, Louisiana. He uses this position to be a positive influence for the gospel. His family is connected to a strong network of Christian friends. If you were to ask Hunter what is most important to him today, he would quickly tell you he has a peace he once did not know and a Father that will never leave him nor forsake him.

Berry Handley

Berry Handley is one of the cofounder's of Team Impact. He stands 6' 7" and weighs over 300 pounds. The guys all refer to him as the "Human Giant." However, his testimony is probably different than most of the testimonies you might hear today. Berry has never used drugs, shot up anything in his veins, and he has never snorted anything up his nose. Berry regularly shares with young people all over the world that he has never tasted Budweiser, the king of beers; but, he has tasted Jesus, the King of Kings.

Berry grew up in a very rough home. Although his mother was a Christian, his father was far from God. His father did not like church and did not want the family to attend. However, Berry's mom would literally sneak him to church.

Berry says, "I remember the first time I went to church. It was right down the street from my house. I sensed a peace the moment I walked into the church. The men greeted me with a smile on their faces as they ushered me to my seat.

"This particular day they had a movie at church about heaven and hell. I couldn't believe it. I was watching a movie at church. As the movie came on the screen, it showed two men's lives, both in their 40's. One was a Christian and one was lost. They both were killed immediately in the movie. One was thrown out of a car going up a mountain, and the other man had a heart attack. The movie tried to show what heaven and hell will be like.

The quality of the film wasn't like today's realistic films, but it changed my life. I came forward and repented of my sins and accepted Christ as my savior."

Berry was only seven years old when he made this decision to trust Christ. At the time, he was the worst reader in his class, a big target for the school bully, and had a terrible home life. These things did not immediately change when Berry made his decision to accept Jesus as his personal Savior. He was still the worst reader in his class, he still regularly was beaten up by the school bully, and he was still living in a difficult environment. Even though life was still tough, Berry knew something was different. At this young age, he had discovered the answer to every one of his problems. His relationship with Jesus gave him new direction and peace.

His mother encouraged him to read his Bible out loud to become a better reader. He started doing this every morning before school and started memorizing various scriptures. Quickly this reading accelerated him from being the worst reader in his class to becoming the best reader in his class. He not only started growing spiritually and academically, he also grew about six inches that year and started developing some biceps. As he grew, the school bully left him alone. His growth also enabled him to accelerate athletically. His father was impressed by Berry's growth in athletics but not in the growth in his spiritual life.

Berry prayed for his dad for years. In his first year of ministry almost 25 years ago, his father came to an event in Chicago to see the team doing feats of strength at a large church. His dad quickly showed interest in the athletes. As they shared their testimonies, Berry's dad received Jesus as his Lord and Savior.

When Berry has the opportunity to share his story, he always says, "My testimony is a testimony of God's keeping power. I accepted Christ at a young age, and I've lived for the Lord my entire life. The Bible says if you commit your ways to God, God will cause you to succeed, and that's exactly what happened in my life. My life has been blessed because I've allowed God to be Lord of all." (Galatians 2:20).

Trey Talley

Trey Talley regularly shares his salvation experience in churches all over the world. Listen to the simple truth of a changed life as it unfolds.

"As far as I know, I never missed a single day of church through all of my childhood years. I praise God for parents that made sure of this. There were absolutely no excuses. Rain, sleet, hail, tornado, tsunami, or sickness could not keep us away.

"Being raised in the church allowed me the opportunity to acquire a lot of Biblical information. I knew about Noah and the Ark, Abraham, Moses, and the stories about Jesus. I knew that Jesus was born, lived, died, and rose from the grave. I not only learned this information but believed all of it to be true. I tried to apply these lessons to my life and be a good kid. I even said my prayers every night before I went to bed.

"Surely this would be enough right? What more could I do? I went to church, knew the Bible stories, said my prayers, and tried to be nice to people. If you were to ask me if I was going to Heaven, I would have said 'Of Course!'

"However, that changed one day when I was nine years old. I was sitting with my friends on the fourth row of Beech Street Baptist Church listening to a revival preacher preach. I don't remember everything that he was preaching about that day, but I do know that he was talking about what it means to be truly saved.

"Prior to this point, I believed everything was okay between God and me. I just assumed that I was on my way to Heaven. But as I sat there listening to this clear message about sin, the punishment of sin, and what Jesus Christ had accomplished, I fell under extreme conviction.

"It was a gut wrenching awakening to my status before God as a sinner. Now, I know you might be thinking, 'You were only nine. How bad could you have really been?'

"I understand that point; however, the problem was not an individual sin that I had committed but that I was a sinner before a Holy God. I felt totally exposed for who I was and conviction sank in like never before. Looking back, I could relate to Adam and Eve. After they sinned, they tried to hide themselves from God because they were ashamed and knew something was not right.

"God was working on me in a special way that day. It was as if God had turned on a search light, and it was now shining on me with all of its brilliance. I was exposed, and now revealed for what I really was, a sinner against God Almighty.

"I made it through the church service not talking to anyone about what was going on. But, I was miserable inside, and I couldn't shake it. When we got back to our house, I went to my room, shut the door, and wept like a little baby.

"Finally, my mother came back to check on me. All she said was 'What's wrong?'

"I tried to compose myself but couldn't, and I fell apart all over again. My mom, realizing what was going on, helped me understand that the only way to be forgiven was by receiving Jesus Christ as my Savior.

"With my mom at my side, kneeling beside my bed, I surrendered, trusted, and believed on Jesus Christ, by grace through faith, for my salvation. I praise God for searching me out, showing me for the sinner that I was, and rescuing me as only He can. Thank you Jesus for saving my soul!"

Mark Minter

Marc Minter is one of our younger team members. He is now married, has an incredible young boy, and resides in Texas. Enjoy his story as he tells it to you.

"I grew up going to church all the time with my mother and my brother. My mom was a single parent who tried her best to expose her two sons to as much church as possible. Life outside of church was different, however. It seemed that the people and things I liked most were nowhere near a church. I loved sports and competition, playing and fighting, and none of these things seemed to be admired in the least by those I encountered at the church.

"I did long for the idea of something or someone bigger than myself. I wanted to understand what my purpose was for existence and what gave me value as a person.

"I chased the dream of becoming an accomplished athlete. I did not climb to the highest level, but I did go as far as I had hoped I would. I became a college football player, and it seemed that the dream had come true.

"Surprisingly, my mind was still plagued with the questions, which I never really answered. Athletic ability, notoriety and relative success were no comfort to me knowing that these things were superficial. None of these would assist me when a loved one died. Not one would come to my aid when I faced a real crisis. The real crisis came when I considered the reality of my sin.

"Sin was something I had heard about in church but never quite understood until I was 19 years old. During my second year of college, I was drawn to ideas that I had not thought about before. If there is a God and He has given rules to follow, would there be a punishment for rebellion? I knew that I had not followed any of the rules. I knew that the punishment must be big for me, but I did not know the half of it.

"For the first time, I started reading the Bible my mother gave to me as a young boy. I read about a Holy God. My eyes began to open to the reality of a perfect, just Judge who would judge my sin. The Bible says in Romans 6:23, 'The wages of sin is death.'

"Simply, my sinfulness deserves the punishment of death (death, not just physical but spiritual). I realized that sin equals punishment and that was not a happy thought for me, because I had sinned…a lot.

"That was not the final word. You see, the rest of Romans 6:23 says, "…But the free gift of God is eternal life through Jesus Christ our Lord."

"I had heard about Jesus before, but I learned that Jesus was God's gift to sinners. I learned that Jesus was the One who had been born without sin; He had lived a perfect life and died a terrible death. His death puzzled me, until I understood what it meant that He died for me. God poured out the judgment, which I deserve, on Jesus Christ as a sacrifice in my place. I live because He died. As I understood this truth for the first time, I trusted Jesus Christ to save me forever.

"There were no fireworks, no bells, and no bright shining lights. Yet, there has been a very significant change in my heart and life since Jesus Christ transformed me. Where once there was only selfish desire and rebellion against God, I now find myself wanting to please God and submit to His authority. I notice the real hunger for reading and understanding God's Word like never before. Sure, I still mess up, and many times I still do things that I know are wrong. Yet, I recognize that it is not my goodness or righteousness that makes God love me, but it is because of the person and work of Jesus Christ that I have the hope of paradise forever."

Shonn Keels

I grew up in a very religious home. My mom and dad took our family to church every week. I often attended church on Wednesday evenings, Sunday mornings, and Sunday nights. I learned all the songs, memorized many verses, knew when to stand up, sit down, kneel, and anything else that was expected of me while participating in our weekly religious routine. Even though I grew up in this religious environment, I felt empty inside.

Because religion did not work, I tried to fill this void with awards. I loved sports and did all I could to excel in each one as the seasons rolled around. I took pride in making the all-star teams, graduating the strongest guy in my high school, and playing on several championship teams. However, I was still empty inside. This emptiness would lead me down a destructive road plagued with drugs and alcohol.

A failed attempt at college, two rehabilitation centers, and a discharge from the United States Navy led me to the point of wanting to commit suicide. I remember it like it was yesterday.

I was standing on top of a Navy ship sometime after midnight. It was an extremely dark night. I remember thinking if I jump off of this ship, no one will miss me for at least a few hours, until those on duty change watch stations. I knew even as a rescue swimmer I would not last long out in the open Pacific that late at night and it would be hours until daylight.

I had it planned and was ready to end it all and then it happened. God would remind me of a song I heard in a little country church at a vacation Bible school, "Jesus loves me this I know." This little song and the truth it reminded me of would cause me to cry out to God for forgiveness. For the first time in my life, I cried out a sincere prayer asking God to change me from the inside out and to give me a new shot at life.

Since that night, my life has not been the same. God took away my desire to be drunk. He helped me find significance in my relationship with Him. He has blessed me with a wife and two beautiful girls. He has given me the privilege of representing Him all over the world. I no longer worry about what a day holds because I truly know the One who holds the day. The emptiness is gone. I live with purpose and walk in a peace I once did not know. And most of all, He has given me the assurance when I die I will live with Him forever in a real place called heaven.

Your Name Here

Let me encourage you now to prayerfully put your story on paper. Most of these testimonies were shared in the third person. Be sure to write yours in the first person to prepare you for sharing it with others. Practice telling it to a close Christian friend.

Then, you will have positioned yourself to follow the instructions of the Apostle Peter: "Always be prepared to give an answer to everyone who asks you to give the reason for the hope that you have." (1 Peter 3:15).

Remember, when writing your story do not use big church words. Write in a language that will be familiar to your unchurched friends. As you write this way, you will surely learn to speak this way.

Do not wait to do this exercise. Please close the book now, pray and ask God to guide your pen as you put your story on paper. When finished, grab a friend and share with them what you are doing. You can do it! Your lost friends are counting on you, and God has given you all the resources you need.

CHAPTER 5

HOLD THE ROPE
THROUGH
INTERRUPTIONS

The small church in New Zealand where we were holding our crusade was unable to host our event in the actual church building. As a result, they rented out a large sports complex that could hold more people. We were backstage getting ready when our crusade manager told us the place was completely packed. He then told us there were three young boys who were not being allowed into the crusade. Next, he told us the management from the sports complex were the ones who were denying the young men access.

Immediately, we went to talk to the manager and asked him to allow the young boys into our event. The manager was very apologetic, but he explained to us he could not allow them entrance. He told us that those boys had been banned from the complex because they were troublemakers. Furthermore, he explained that they had stolen items and had even vandalized the building.

We knew our begging was in vain. He was not going to let them in. The program was about to start, but I knew this interruption was for a reason. As fast as I could, I asked one of the other team members, Siolo, to grab a phone book and follow me outside.

The three young delinquents sat on a concrete bench just outside of the front door. After talking with them for a few minutes, I recognized that the manager's assessment of these young men was accurate. Their language was littered with profanity, and their behavior was rude.

Trying to engage them, I asked if they would like to see something pretty cool. Not wanting to seem too anxious, they merely nodded their heads that they would.

I then asked, "Do you think my buddy Siolo can rip this phone book in half?"

One of the boys immediately asked to see the phone book because he was certain it had been "fixed" in some way. After giving the phone book a thorough inspection he merely said, "No way."

Siolo grabbed the 800 page phone book and ripped it right down the middle like a single sheet of paper. As if on cue, all three of the boys mouths dropped open.

Knowing I had their attention, I briefly shared my testimony. I then asked them if they would like to trust Jesus as their Lord and Savior. With absolute sincerity, they each audibly said "Yes." Next, I prayed with them and for them. Afterward, Siolo and I welcomed our new brothers in Christ into the Family of God.

The time we spent with those boys was an interruption to our normal pre-service preparation. Do you hold the rope and get others close to Jesus when you are interrupted? Jesus was never too busy to do the miraculous. Matthew 9:14-26 says:

> Then John's disciples came and asked him, "How is it that we and the Pharisees fast, but your disciples do not fast?"
>
> Jesus answered, "How can the guests of the bridegroom mourn while he is with them? The time will come when the bridegroom will be taken from them; then they will fast. No one sews a patch of unshrunk cloth on an old garment, for the patch will pull away from the garment, making the tear worse. Neither do men pour new wine into old wineskins. If they do, the skins will burst, the wine will run out and the wineskins will be ruined. No, they pour new wine into new wineskins, and both are preserved.
>
> While he was saying this, a ruler came and knelt before him and said, "My daughter has just

died. But come and put your hand on her, and she will live."

Jesus got up and went with him, and so did his disciples. Just then a woman who had been subject to bleeding for twelve years came up behind him and touched the edge of his cloak.

She said to herself, "If I only touch his cloak, I will be healed."

Jesus turned and saw her.

"Take heart, daughter," he said. "Your faith has healed you." And the woman was healed from that moment.

When Jesus entered the ruler's house and saw the flute players and the noisy crowd, he said, "Go away. The girl is not dead but asleep." But they laughed at him. After the crowd had been put outside, he went in and took the girl by the hand, and she got up. News of this spread through all that region.

This is really an amazing account. Jesus is asked why He and his disciples do not fast. Jesus is basically in the middle of a sermon, explaining that new wine must be put in new wineskins. All of a sudden, in the middle of His teaching, a ruler comes and asks Him to come and raise his daughter from the dead. Unfazed, Jesus goes to fulfill his request. Unbelievably, on His way to heal the little girl, He heals another woman who was suffering from a discharge of blood. Jesus was never too busy to do the miraculous for those in need.

I am often busy with my ministry schedule. I am afraid that in my effort to stay on my schedule, I often disregard God's schedule. The greatest miracle is not a little girl being revived. Instead, it is when you and I hold the rope and people are made spiritually alive.

In 1995, I was playing professional football in the Canadian Football League. I tried to be a good witness to my teammates, and I would often invite them to my church. The Senior Pastor was an unbelievable evangelist, and the Gospel was clearly presented during every service. Over a period of weeks, I had invited a teammate of mine named Dave. He said he would go many times, but he always seemed to back out at the last minute. Finally, one Sunday morning, my teammate came to church and sat with me and my family. I was so anxious to hear which evangelistic message my pastor was going to deliver that would, in my mind, compel my friend to get saved.

This particular morning my pastor chose to teach on the Lord's Supper. The teaching was magnificent and sound; however, in my opinion, not particularly evangelistic. Pastor explained that after we took the Lord's Supper, we were free to leave.

I was livid. I had brought my friend here to get saved. Where was the big emotional invitation? Just when I was ready to scream, I heard the Pastor say, "The only way you can partake of the Lord's Supper is if you are a member of the Body of Christ." He continued, "In fact, if you do not know Jesus as your Lord and Savior raise your hand." There was no "heads bowed and eyes closed." He just expected whoever was not saved to raise his hand with everyone looking. In my flesh, I was thinking this will not work.

I then glanced to my right and my teammate, all 6 foot 5 of him, had his enormous hand raised in the air. Pastor then looked at me and said, "Jeff why don't you pray with him to receive Christ." Pastor then looked at the other thousand people in attendance and asked them to be in an attitude of prayer until we were finished. I looked at my buddy, and he was holding back tears. He explained that he wanted to know Christ in a relationship and on the spot, we prayed together.

After we were through, my teammate and I took the Lord's Supper together for the first time as brothers in Christ.

The pastor was willing to hold the rope and get my friend close to Jesus even though this is not how the typical invitation was done. Nevertheless, the pastor was tuned into God's timing.

Jesus was so willing to be interrupted to touch those in need. Jesus was always available. In fact, people would often bring people to Him while he was traveling. Mark 6:53-56 says:

> When they had crossed over, they landed at Gennesaret and anchored there. As soon as they

got out of the boat, people recognized Jesus. They ran throughout that whole region and carried the sick on mats to wherever they heard he was. And wherever he went—into villages, towns or countryside—they placed the sick in the marketplaces. They begged him to let them touch even the edge of his cloak, and all who touched him were healed.

People that know me are aware that I love to witness to people. I have had people call me to come over to their house if they are conversing with Jehovah's Witnesses or Latter Day Saints, and they are experiencing trouble. Holding the rope means that you are willing to compromise your schedule for the sake of the gospel.

Often, I wonder who God wants me to witness to when I am stuck in an airport because of a weather delay. God does not make mistakes. There is not a single maverick molecule. God is in complete control. God does not only justify the end of salvation but also the means to that end. What looks like an interruption to you is instead God's carefully orchestrated plan.

I love witnessing on airplanes. I do not sit in first class; I sit in coach class. I figure, if I am going to sit next to you and halfway in your seat, I might as well witness to you. I contend that the person sitting next to me was sent there by God. For at least an hour, I can witness to the person next to me, and they cannot go anywhere. Yes, God knew before the foundations of the earth that this person would sit next to me so that I could share the Good News of His Son Jesus. If we truly saw interruptions as divinely scheduled events, I think we would be more willing to hold the rope and share Jesus.

I was traveling from my hotel, a number of years ago, on my way to an outreach. Trey, one of the members of Team Impact, was driving his car, and I was in the passenger seat. In the back seat was another team member, Guy Earle. Guy used to play football in the NFL and is about 6 foot 6 inches tall and weighs over 300 pounds.

We were on our way to church to start the set up process which takes well over an hour. The roads were a little wet from an afternoon rain, but it was of no great concern. As we approached a cross street, traveling at about 50 mph, we noticed a car nearing a stop sign to our immediate right. Without warning, the car ran through the stop sign, and then the driver came to a complete stop right in front of us as he froze in panic. Trey slammed on his brakes but it was too late. My face slammed into the air bag, and my entire body shook with the extraordinary violence of the collision.

I was hit pretty hard playing pro football, but nothing has come close to the shock I felt at the very core of my being. Immediately, the car began to fill up with smoke and we knew that we should get out as fast as possible. Trey jumped out of the driver's side door, but my door was so badly dented that I could not force it open. As a result, I climbed across the console and out Trey's door. We then forced Guy's door open and helped him out. We were unbelievably surprised as we inspected each other for any visible injuries and there were none. No one was bleeding and there was not a single broken bone.

Next, our attention was brought to the young man who was in the car that we struck. The driver, a seventeen year old boy, had his head against the steering wheel with his eyes closed. I was sure he was dead. However, as I ran up to the car, I could see that he was crying and distraught but uninjured. We helped him out of the car and sat him on what was left of the hood of his car.

Within ten minutes a police officer arrived on the scene and began to perform his thorough investigation. He asked who was driving. Trey acknowledged that it was his car and began to explain how the accident happened. I explained that I was in the front passenger seat. He then asked who was sitting in the backseat and we pointed to the massive Guy Earle. Wanting more information, the officer asked if he was sitting in the back right or back left seat. I laughed and said, "Sir, he is 6'6"… 300 pounds… he was sitting in the entire back seat."

I gave a quick glance over to the driver of the car we hit. The young man was still sitting on the hood of his car with a completely dejected look on his face. I immediately made my way over to the teenage boy and once again asked him if he was ok. He explained to me that the car he wrecked was his mother's and he was going to be in serious trouble. I sympathized, but quickly reassured him, she would be happy that he was not hurt. I then looked him in the eyes and said, "Can I please pray for you?" He nodded his head, and I prayed a simple prayer of thanks, that our lives had been spared. As we concluded our prayer, I told him about Team Impact and invited him to the program that would start in about an hour. He told me he would come if he could, and I assured him that seats would be saved on the front row if he should choose to show up.

Within five minutes, someone showed up in a church van to take us to the program so we could begin the arduous set-up process. We finished setting up the last break with about fifteen minutes to spare. We quickly changed into our uniforms, and were just about to be introduced, when I saw the young man who drove the car we collided into walk in the church. He was coming in the church with his friend he went to school with. The guys from Team Impact and I ran over to him and shook his hand to welcome him. We then had an usher show him to the seats we had reserved for him on the front row.

The two teenage boys cheered for us as we broke the bats, smashed the bricks, and exploded the hot water bottle. More importantly, as the Gospel was preached, both young men were being visibly convicted. At the end of the program, people across the sanctuary were asked to raise their hands if they wanted to yield their lives to Jesus Christ and be born again. I held back tears, as I looked on the front row and saw the young man who hours earlier had totaled his car, now raise his hand in total surrender to Christ. Though this young man had walked in dead in his trespasses, he would walk out alive in Christ.

God orchestrated this divine interruption before time began. God knew that even an accident could be used as an opportunity to hold the rope and get a young man close to Jesus.

CHAPTER 6

HOLD THE ROPE IN YOUR LOCAL CHURCH

T he Church is the visual representation of Jesus Christ in the world today. She stands mightily as the steward of the greatest story ever told. It is up to her to share the glorious gospel of the Lord Jesus Christ with the whole human race. This is God's plan! And if you have called upon Jesus Christ as Lord and Savior, you are an integral part of the church. You are an important part of God's plan. Your unique gifts and talents are vital to the overall mission of the church to get people close to Jesus.

Imagine what it could have been like when Jesus ascended back into heaven. Imagine the angels all gathered around to worship the risen Lord. As they took notice of His nail-scarred hands and feet, the scars around his brow, the hole in his side, and the scars all over his body, an angel spoke up, "Lord, surely the whole world knows of the great sacrifice you have made for them?"

Jesus replied, "No, they do not all know."

The angel inquires, "But Lord, you paid such a great price. Surely all the world knows."

Jesus answers, "No, only a few in Jerusalem know of my sacrifice."

The angel then asks, "How will the world know if only a few in Jerusalem know?"

Jesus says confidently, "I have commissioned those in Jerusalem to tell others, who will then tell others, who will then tell others and others until all the world knows of the great price I have paid for the sins of all who believe?"

The angel humbly responds, "Lord, I have witnessed the disobedience of your people in the past. Please tell us you have made other plans."

Jesus declares, "No, I have made no other plans. I am counting on the Church!"

Clearly God is depending on the Church to reach the world with the gospel of Christ. He has made no other plans. The Church is His change agent in the world. It is both the responsibility and the privilege of the Church to hold the rope and get people close to Jesus.

The Church has and will continue to be the steward of the timeless message of the gospel. Please remember the Church is not the building on the corner with a steeple on the top. She is made up of all who have called on the name of the Lord Jesus and received salvation through faith in His finished work. If this is you, God has invited and equipped you to hold the rope and get your friends close to Jesus.

What are you doing to help the mission of your local church move forward? Week after week, month after month, and year after year what are you doing to hold the rope in your local church so others have the opportunity to experience authentic Christian community, hear the gospel preached, learn what it means to know God personally, and play a part in making him known? Jesus is counting on the Church, and the Bible clearly teaches you are an important part of the Church.

When I was serving as a senior pastor, we hosted a Team Impact crusade about every 18 months. Each time we held a crusade, our leadership teams recruited large numbers of volunteers to serve. The teams recruited people to park cars, greet at the doors, usher, provide meals, work on stage, counsel, assist in baptisms, pray, get materials, market the event, keep the nursery, and other necessary things. More than 100 people would come out to serve for the week. They loved it.

Team Impact members would roll into town and go from school to school to motivate students to make responsible decisions and then present the gospel in the evening programs. We would see literally 400 or more each year make decisions for Christ and baptize as many as 100 in the 5 nights.

Now, who was responsible for holding the rope for these 400 people so they could get close to Jesus? Was it the Team Impact members? Or was it the pastoral staff who came up with the idea of having the event? Could it have been the prayer team, the counselors, or one of the other teams who made it possible to pull off such an event?

The answer to the question is simple: Yes. It was all of them, and everyone else who served in any area to make the event possible. Everyone played a part in holding the rope so more than 400 people could get close to Jesus.

Together is how the Church operates. This is why the Bible refers to the church as a body. Everybody is made up of parts and all parts are important. The hand cannot function as an eye and neither can the eye function as a hand; however, together, with all of the other body parts, the eye and the hand help make the body function at its optimal level. And so it is with the Church. Although we all possess different gifts, abilities, and talents, God uses us together to hold the rope and get people close to Jesus.

There was a plumber in our church who claimed he had no special abilities. He came to church and loved it but believed he did not have what it takes to play apart in helping hold the rope to get people close to Jesus. Once, I talked to our leadership team about a desire to build a coffee shop in our lobby to serve people as they were coming into our weekend experiences. They agreed this would help provide the atmosphere we desired to create. We felt like a cup of Java and/or a doughnut might help these spiritual seekers feel comfortable in an unfamiliar spiritual climate.

I asked the plumber if he would manage and maintain our coffee shop. I explained this would require him to keep it stocked, clean, and full of volunteers. He agreed this was something he could do. Many times I would read through the response cards from our weekend experiences and receive comments about how awesome it was to have a coffee shop.

I remember over hearing someone in the gym who was not very fond of church in general because of a bad experience he had as a child, but the man felt at home at our church. He had originally visited our church because a member told him that our church had a casual atmosphere where he could get a cup of coffee and drink it while the guy was giving "his speech."

Many who were far from God loved the casual atmosphere the coffee shop helped create and were willing to come back week after week to hear challenging messages. Some of them would eventually surrender their lives to Jesus. The plumber now understands he is an integral part in the rope holding equation. How about you? What part are you playing to hold the rope in your local church?

Ralph came by my church one day and told me about his adult son Dave, and his desire to serve in our children's ministry. He also explained that Dave had a mental disability. He brought references from his former church and assured me Dave's challenges would cause no problems for our ministry. We immediately honored the request, and Dave quickly got involved in our children's ministry.

He volunteered with a team at our children's welcome center. His childlike mind brought such enthusiasm to our welcome center. He loved the children, and the children loved him. He eventually helped in the classrooms assisting the teachers with the little ones as they worked on classroom projects.

Dave also worked at a local grocery store bagging groceries. Our church was one of the largest churches in the area, and many of our members shopped at this store. I remember more than once hearing children yell out from their seat in their buggies, "Hey mom, there's Mr. Dave." Dave was an integral part in helping our church hold the rope and get people close to Jesus.

There are countless other stories of real people who are holding the rope week after week in their local churches. However, it is sad some do not hold the rope because they are unsure how they fit on the team. Trust me. You fit. Just like the above testimonies, you are an integral part of the team.

If you have not yet found your place, let me recommend you start holding the rope in some way in your church today. Go to your church leadership and tell them of your desire to help hold the rope. Your leadership will help you find your place. When you begin to help hold the rope in your church, you will be helping men and women and boys and girls get close to Jesus. This will not only change their lives. It will change your life too!

Sometimes holding the rope in your local church is as simple as asking someone to attend church with you.

This is what happened to Team Impact member Ron Waterman. His dad would not give up on him. His dad lovingly and regularly invited Ron to attend weekend services with him. Finally, Ron accepted his father's invitation and got close enough to Jesus for his life to be changed. Ron tells the story. "I recently had lunch with a former student of mine from one of the first years I taught at Greeley West High School. I sat and listened to my friend as he went on and on about how much he admired and looked up to me. He started with letting me know how cool it was to have a teacher who was a Mr. Colorado Bodybuilder and how he loved that in his senior year he was able to watch me on Television in the "Ultimate Fighting Championships" (UFC) as a top heavyweight contender. He went on to speak of the excitement he felt to know me because of the contract I was given to compete in the WWF, now the WWE, as a professional wrestler. He told me how excited he was to be able to play my character on a video game on PlayStation.

"It was interesting to listen to an outsider piece my life together into a fairytale existence. One that sounded like it belonged on one of the lifestyles of the rich and famous episodes. I could only chuckle to myself as I realized the cost and sacrifice some of these worldly achievements had on my life. One thing I realized many years ago is that all the fame, all the glory, and all of the money in the world cannot buy happiness, cannot buy your soul, and certainly cannot buy you an eternity in heaven!

"Although I did have chapters of my life that may have seemed glorious to many and a lifestyle that only few can say they lived, it was far from what I would consider a life filled with peace and joy like the Lord wants for us. At 12 years of age, my parents divorced. I took it hard as most kids do. Blame and guilt consumed me for years. The pain caused me to grow quiet and independent. I developed a mindset that I could do everything myself if I just worked hard enough.

"During this time in my life, sports became a passion. I sought refuge in the heat of competition. I excelled in wrestling and became a top competitor in the state of Colorado as a senior in high school. I was offered a wrestling scholarship to a major college. My desire to succeed led me to become one of the best heavyweight wrestlers in the nation my senior year of college.

"During this journey if someone were to ask me if I was a Christian I would have without hesitation told them, 'Of course.' I believed I was a Christian. After all, I used to go to church with my parents as a kid and was confirmed in the Lutheran Church. I knew who God was.

"I now realize, while I may have been religious, I did not have a relationship with God. As a young adult I drifted away from church. I was too busy and did not see the need. I figured I lived a better life than most of my friends and did a lot of good things. I believed I was ok because I was a good person.

"Years went by as I tried to climb the ladder of success and find fulfillment in my life. As I lived life on my own, pursuing this elusive success, my life quickly spiraled downward to the point of almost giving up. I could never find the peace and joy in life I was looking for. My father had been asking me to attend church with him for some time; but, as always, I was too busy and had too many things going on to take a couple of hours out of my weekend for church.

"My life had become so out of control that one Sunday morning, I finally gave in and accepted my father's invitation to church. It was as if he had filled the pastor in that day because I felt the sermon was directed right at me! Every word out of his mouth poignantly spoke to the issues that were overwhelming my life.

"On that day at church, I felt something inside me I had never felt before. I did not know what it was, but I did know I needed it. I continued to attend church with my dad. A couple of weeks later, I realized I needed help and could not do this thing called life alone anymore regardless of how tough I thought I was.

"After listening to the pastor's message this Sunday, during the response time, he gave a very simple yet direct invitation. I knew, at that moment, he was speaking to me. I knew it was me who needed to accept Christ. I surrendered my life to Jesus. I walked forward with tears in my eyes, and for the first time in my life, sensed the weight of the world had just been lifted off of my back and placed on the one who died for me, Jesus. On that day many questions surrounding my life were answered, many problems were lifted, and most of all, I experienced a peace I never knew.

"God has truly made me a new creation. I am not the same Ron Waterman any more. Jesus lives in me and I want everyone I come in contact with to see that! Now, as a Christian, I still face challenges. Life is still full of obstacles. However, I do not have to face them alone. For God said, 'Never will I leave you, never will I forsake you.' (Hebrews 13:5).

"Jesus has the answers to my problems and yours. Sometimes we just need to be silent and listen.

"One of my favorite verses in the Bible comes from John 10:10. 'A thief comes to kill, steal and destroy, but I have come so you may have life and have it to the full.'

"One thing that brings me to my knees every day of my life is God's grace. The fact that he came into my life after 32 years of my bad choices and the terrible things I did still overwhelms me. Think about it, after 32 years of turning my back on God, He would extend His grace and mercy to me. He would remove the baggage off my back and put it on His own. What an awesome God!

"One of the last things my young friend told me as we sat and ate lunch that day was the thing that most impressed him about my life. He said that after all you have achieved, you now travel around the world to tell people about Jesus Christ and what He did for your life and what He can do for others. All the accolades meant nothing to me, but when he said that, it made me so proud to know I am making a difference."

There is power in the ask! Go ahead and invite someone today. Do not push, just ask! Remember to practice what you have learned so far in this book. Love your friends, get involved in their lives, and then invite them to join you for a weekend service. And do not forget to pray. God just might use you to hold the rope and get them close enough to Jesus for their lives to be changed!

CHAPTER 7

HOLD THE ROPE
THROUGH
APOLOGETICS

The church is called to hold the rope for others by giving a clear and accurate Biblical explanation of who Jesus is. The name of Jesus is used in so many ways by so many people that we must clearly define our terms. Was Jesus a mere man? Was he just a prophet?

The world must get from the church a clear, cogent answer that is not based on feelings or experiences but based on God's Word.

There is a story of an arrogant Captain of a Navy Battleship. He was very young to be in charge of an entire ship, so he often felt insecure. As a result, to show that he was the one in charge, he barked orders loudly and expected immediate obedience.

One day, a dense fog set in as the battleship cruised the shoreline. All of the sudden, in the distance, the Captain saw the light of an apparent ship directly in his path. As he was unable to establish radio contact with the fast approaching light, he ordered the subordinate officer to flash, by spotlight, the following message in Morse Code: "Alter your course 20 degrees west."

Immediately, by a series of pulsing lights, the message flashed, "No, you alter your course 20 degrees east."

Not used to being disobeyed, the captain was angry. He yelled to his officer, "You flash this message, 'This is Captain Johnson, I order you to alter your course 20 degrees west.'"

"No Captain, you alter your course 20 degrees east.

Now the captain was livid and he yelled at the top of his voice, "You flash this message, 'This is Captain Johnson and this is a battleship. Immediately alter your course 20 degrees west.'"

And once again the response was immediate from the approaching light, as the final message was delivered, "This is a lighthouse, alter your course 20 degrees east."

The Bible is a lighthouse. We cannot alter who Jesus is based upon what our feelings or even what some teacher says is true. Jesus must be defined by who God's Word says He is. The world deserves a Jesus that is defined by his Holy Word.

In Acts 8:30-35, a man named Philip is instructed to go to a particular place by an angel of the Lord. There,

Philip encounters an Ethiopian eunuch who was an important official. The eunuch was reading a passage out of the book of Isaiah. He asks Philip, "How can I understand this passage unless someone explains it to me?"

I believe there is a questioning world grasping to understand God's Word, and they, like the eunuch, are begging for someone to explain it to them. We must be equipped to explain who Jesus is.

So who was the historical Jesus? The Bible declares that Jesus Christ was the Son of God and God the Son. He was the theoantropos – the God man. Jesus was 100% God and 100% man. We as Bible believing Christians embrace ontological monotheism. In other words, God in His very essence or nature is one. The equivalent of John 3:16 for the Old Testament Jew was Deuteronomy 6:4, which says, "Hear O Israel the Lord our God the Lord is one." There is one God who reveals himself in three co-eternal, eternally distinct persons.

Many cults today deny the deity of Jesus Christ. However, Scripture clearly affirms that Jesus is God. John 1:1 says, "In the beginning was the Word, and the Word was with God, and the Word was God."

The Apostle Paul, under the inspiration of the Holy Spirit, in Philippians 2:6-7 says, "Who, being in very nature God, did not consider equality with God something to be grasped, but made himself nothing, taking the very nature of a servant, being made in human likeness."

Finally, Jesus applies the name of deity to Himself in John 8:58 when He says, "'I tell you the truth,' Jesus answered, 'before Abraham was born, I am!'"

Those are just a few of the many Biblical examples that acknowledge the deity of Christ. The purpose of this chapter is not to replace a systematic theology textbook.

Nevertheless, from just the few verses I have mentioned, one cannot walk away from the discussion and say Jesus was a mere man. C.S. Lewis asserted that Jesus was either a liar, a lunatic, or Lord. There is no fence to straddle. There is no middle ground. Jesus, without a doubt, claimed to be God.

You may be asking yourself, "Why is it so important that Jesus was indeed 'the image of the invisible God?'" (Colossians 1:15). This doctrine is not tangential or secondary to our faith; it is essential to our understanding of God.

The Bible declares everyone of us, because of the fall of Adam and Eve, is born with a sinful nature. We know how to do wrong from birth.

When my son Graham was 1 year old, he always wanted to play with his DVDs that we kept in a cabinet under the TV. However, I would not let him play with his DVDs because he would scratch them, and I knew that someday he would break one. I would tell him no, but he was unable to resist the temptation.

Eventually, I put child locks on those cabinets. These locks were the kind that would only allow the cabinet to open an inch or two max. However, Graham learned in a very short time, that if he banged the cabinet as hard as he could, 20 times in a row, he could bust the lock open.

I would be on the couch watching his every move. After he forced the cabinet open, he would freeze for about 5 seconds. Ever so slowly, he would begin to inch his hand toward the DVDs.

Now I'm not able to ascertain the thoughts of a toddler, but I always imagined he was thinking something like, "If I move slow enough, the old man will not even know that I am moving."

Once he reached the DVD with his plump fingers, he would grasp it and run! He completely understood he wanted the DVD. He also knew that it was forbidden. Graham did not have to be taught how to do that which is wrong because he was born with a sinful nature.

As a sinful man, I was an enemy of God from birth. Because I have been born again, the righteousness of Christ has been imputed to me. The apostle Paul says it this way in I Corinthians 15:21-22, "For since death came through a man, the resurrection of the dead comes also through a man. For as in Adam all die, so in Christ all will be made alive."

It is paramount that we communicate that Jesus was born of a virgin. Jesus, unlike you and me, was born without original sin. In addition, Jesus was the perfect sin sacrifice, because He never committed a single sin. The deity of Christ, His virgin birth, His literal resurrection, and His full atonement on the cross of Calvary are not issues that only have their place in the classrooms of seminary.

I love to witness to all sorts of people. I particularly have a passion to witness to people who are in non-Christian cults such as Jehovah's Witness or Latter Day Saints (Mormons). In fact, I have spent countless hours studying the Bible so that when I encounter these people I can hold the rope and get them close to the Jesus of the Bible. In an attempt to be the best witness I can be, I will even study their material to familiarize myself with the arguments I will encounter.

Most Christians probably do not need to study what non-Christians embrace as truth. Instead, every Christian needs to know their own personal beliefs based on the Holy Bible.

When the US Government hires experts to identify counterfeit money, they do not show them all sorts of different fake money. Instead, they show them the real money. They want the experts to be so familiar with the real thing that, when a counterfeit is handed to them, they recognize it instantaneously. Our faith should be the same. Our knowledge of who Jesus is should be so strong that when someone comes to us with a counterfeit it is immediately recognized as bogus.

The sole purpose of being equipped to hold the rope and present the true Jesus is not to win an argument. Instead, the end result is to win a soul. Being prepared with the answer is the duty of every Bible believing Christian who wants to get others close to Jesus.

A few years ago, I was in Los Angeles for a crusade. On this particular Saturday, we were helping with a food drop with our friend Larry Jones and his organization,

Feed the Children. Our job this particular day was to help take boxes of food off the back of a semi truck trailer. From there, we would carry the food to the cars of the people who were in need.

I saw two young men riding by on bicycles. Because of their familiar dress, white shirts, ties, and name tags, I recognized that these two young men were Mormons. Without hesitating I jumped from the back of the truck, grabbed a Bible, and hollered at the two boys, "Please stop."

I am guessing they were really shocked to see a 300 pound man running toward them with a Bible in his hand. Most of the time when they go from door to door, people slam the door in their face. Suddenly, they were being confronted with someone who desperately wanted to talk to them.

If you do not know much about the Mormon religion they are polytheistic. They embrace a principle called "eternal progression." This promise states that God was once a man, and he progressed into a God. In fact, most LDS missionaries have memorized a couplet made famous by Brigham Young, which states, "As man is now God once was, as God is now man may become."

The first thing I told these two young Mormon missionaries, after I applauded their commitment to their religion, was that the difference between LDS and Christians was Christians believe in one God, and Mormons believe in multiple gods. At first they disagreed and said they only believe in one god as well. I then recited the famous couplet by Brigham Young and asked them to explain eternal progression.

They realized I knew what Mormons believed and then they modified their statement of belief in "one god" to "only one god for this Earth." They admitted that their hope was to someday attain god status.

Once we identified an important difference in our beliefs, I began to give them Scripture passages which state there is only "One God." One passage that seemed to cause them to take a fresh look at the beliefs they held so dear was Isaiah 44:6 which says, "This is what the Lord says, Isreal's King and Redeemer the Lord Almighty; I am the first and I am the last, apart from me there is no God."

Then to leave no doubt there is only one God Isaiah writes in Chapter 44:8b, "You are my witnesses, is there any Rock besides me? No, there is no other Rock, I know not one."

One of the young men I was speaking to wanted to leave. However, the other young man was listening intently to every passage I gave him. He did not try to argue, and he had no passages to refute that which I was saying. I will never forget, however, as long as I live, the next question he asked.

With complete sincerity in his voice, he looked me right in the eyes and said, "Jeff, my mom and dad are both Mormons. I have given two years of my life as a missionary in the field. I felt a burning in my chest when I prayed about the Book of Mormon. Why would God let me be deceived?"

"Young man, God would not let you be deceived, and that is why he had you ride by here today so I could tell you the truth of God's Word."

His question was valid. This young Mormon missionary, like the Ethiopian eunuch, was asking, "How can I understand who Jesus is unless someone explains it to me?"

Here is the challenge: Study God's Word in such a way that when people have questions about the person of Christ you will be able to hold the rope and get them close to the real Jesus.

CHAPTER 8

HOLD THE ROPE
WITH LOVE

I have heard it said that the number one cause of atheism in the world today is the Christian who professes Jesus with his lips but denies Him with his lifestyle. Friend this cannot be the case with you and me. If we truly desire to hold the rope and get our friends close to Jesus, we must learn to live out our faith. Our life must point to Christ in both our actions and attitudes.

This does not mean we have to be perfect, but it does mean the most defining characteristic of our lives should be love. Love will prove to be our best weapon in the war for the salvation of our friends.

In the rest of this chapter we are going to look at Luke 10:25-37 to gain a better understanding of how we are to love.

On one occasion an expert in the law stood up to test Jesus. "Teacher," he asked, "what must I do to inherit eternal life?"

"What is written in the Law?" he replied. "How do you read it?"

He answered: "'Love the Lord your God with all your heart and with all your soul and with all your strength and with all your mind'; and, 'Love your neighbor as yourself.' "You have answered correctly," Jesus replied. "Do this and you will live."

But he wanted to justify himself, so he asked Jesus, "And who is my neighbor?"

In reply Jesus said: "A man was going down from Jerusalem to Jericho, when he fell into the hands of robbers. They stripped him of his clothes, beat him and went away, leaving him half dead. A priest happened to be going down the same road, and when he saw the man, he passed by on the other side. So too, a Levite, when he came to the place and saw him, passed by on the other side. But a Samaritan, as he traveled, came where the man was; and when he saw him, he took pity on him. He went to him and bandaged his wounds, pouring on oil and wine. Then he put the man on his own donkey, took him to an inn and took care of him. The next day he took out two silver coins and gave them to the innkeeper. 'Look after him,' he said, 'and when I return, I will reimburse you for any extra expense you may have.'

"Which of these three do you think was a neighbor to the man who fell into the hands of robbers?"

The expert in the law replied, "The one who had mercy on him."

Jesus told him, "Go and do likewise."

The parable of the Good Samaritan gives us a picture of the love that is to define our lives as fully devoted followers of Christ. There are 3 key descriptions of love found in this passage. Be sure to learn them and live them. By doing so, you will be holding the rope for those in your circle of influence.

The first key description of love in this parable is that love is blind to the things that separate people. Notice first who did not stop and help the person in need: the priest and the Levite. The two religious guys just passed by the injured traveler and did nothing. The two who claimed to know God walked by and offered no assistance to the man in distress. They obviously saw the person in need as an interruption to their schedule. If we are to win souls, we cannot be too busy to lend a helping hand. We cannot go through life looking the other way as those in our circle of influence slip farther and farther into depravity. We must take notice of their desperate position and do what we can to get them close to Jesus.

Who stopped to help? The Samaritan did. The Samaritan saw the person in need as an opportunity to show love, not as an interruption to his schedule. Jesus used the Samaritan in the story to give a glimpse into the depth of the love that is to define the fully devoted follower of Christ. This love is blind to the things that normally separate and divide the human race. In this cultural context, the Samaritan would be the least likely to stop and help a Jew. Jews and Samaritans were different: racially, religiously and culturally. These differences created a great divide between their races. However, Jesus uses the Samaritan in the parable to show that love sees through color, culture and creed. Love has no boundaries. Love builds bridges, not barriers.

When my daughters were 5 and 8 years old, we took them on a cross cultural mission trip to serve in the orphanages of Romania. They were great examples of blind love. When we walked into the first orphanage, the children did not speak English, smelled as if they had not bathed recently and looked very different from our group. However, this did not stop our girls. Before we ever gave the word for them to play with the orphans, they were in the mix of them. It was a humbling experience as a father to see our girls looking past the differences, as if there were none, and loving on these children, as if they had been best friends for years. Even though the orphans did not speak English, and our girls did not speak Romanian, they spoke a common language — love. A love that knew no boundaries! And this love is a language anyone can understand.

In verses 33-34, Jesus shows that a second key description of love is service. Notice the Samaritan got off of his donkey and administered first aid to the helpless victim. He rolled up his sleeves and got his hands dirty.

The Samaritan obviously understood that to love is to personally inconvenience self for the benefit of others. It has been said by many great communicators, "You can serve without loving but you cannot love without serving." This passage certainly communicates this powerful truth.

My father-in-law is a perfect illustration of this key description of love. He is always serving those around him in small practical ways. I have never seen him at the front of a line, and he is always the last one to enter a room because he is holding the door for others to enter. My wife tells of how when her father would take her to the grocery store as a child, it would take them forever to check out because her dad would always allow people to cut in line. He has never known a stranger. Everyone he meets, he treats as if he has known them for a lifetime, and he selflessly puts their needs above his own. His legacy will certainly be one of love for he has and continues to serve others.

The third key description of love found in the parable is sacrifice. In verses 34-35, the Samaritan sacrifices time, energy, and money to help the man in need. After bandaging his wounds, the Samaritan took the injured traveler to a local inn, purchased him a room and some food, and worked it out with the inn manager that his needs would be met. It was obvious from the story the Samaritan had a life. The Samaritan had to leave to take care of some business, but before doing so, he made sure the man would be taken care of at no expense to himself. He went above and beyond the call of duty to ensure the distressed man would be taken care of and safe. Then he promised the inn keeper he would return and repay any added expense that may come up in his absence.

Kevin Dowd and I traveled to Australia together to lead a few Team Impact crusades. Our travel pattern left us in San Francisco for a 10 hour layover. Instead of sitting in the airport the entire time, we took the train downtown to get a workout and to eat. After eating at a pizza shop, we decided to head back to the airport so we did not miss our flight. While walking back to the train, we passed a man who obviously lived on the street. The man was seated on the sidewalk just outside a sub sandwich shop. I honestly did not think much about him. However, Kevin entered the sub shop, purchased a sandwich and a bottle of water, then knelt down and gave it to the man on the street. When the man reached to receive the sandwich, Kevin said to him, "God loves you." Kevin then gave him the sandwich, smiled, and we walked off. I do not know what has happened to the man on the street, but I do know on that day Kevin demonstrated the love Jesus taught about in this parable. He sacrificed a little of his time and resources to show someone God's love. We will do well to do the same.

We can never be so busy or consumed with self that we do not notice those who need to be served. No longer can we see people as interruptions to our schedule. We have been called to live life on a mission, a mission of love—a mission of serving others. After all, serving others will prove to be our highest calling in life.

Dr. Jim Austin is the executive director of the South Carolina Baptist Convention and my former pastor. I remember regularly hearing Pastor Jim say, "We must always be willing to personally inconvenience ourselves for the benefit of others." He not only said this, he modeled it time and time again in very real and practical ways. As a staff, we were not allowed to park on our campus during our weekend services. Pastor Jim led the way as we all parked down the road at a bank to free up spots closer to the church for others. This attitude of servitude should permeate our life and witness. Each time we personally inconvenience ourselves for the benefit of others, we are living like the Samaritan, and God will use this type of a life to get people close to Jesus.

There is no greater investment than to invest into the lives of people. God loves people more than anything. He modeled what this love is to look like when He sacrificed his one and only Son, the Lord Jesus Christ. This sacrifice is a beautiful picture of real love. This love is different than the world's love. It gives and expects nothing in return.

Like musical artists before me, I ask, "What's love got to do with it?" I submit to you, based on the authority of God's Word, love has everything to do with it. As Jesus said in verse 37, "Go and do likewise." Hold the rope with love and watch God work in you and through you to change the lives of those you encounter.

CHAPTER 9

HOLD THE ROPE
WITH JOHN 3:16

There is no magic formula for sharing the gospel. However, the better you are equipped for sharing, the more God will use you to hold the rope and get your friends close to Jesus. Learning a method or two will help you feel more comfortable as you begin to share the life changing message with your friend who is far from God. Do not be scared.

If your friend does not accept Christ, do not give up on him. Continue to love him and be the best friend you can possibly be to him. Do not take his non-responsiveness to the gospel personally.

It is not your responsibility to save your friend. You have been commissioned to love him and to share the gospel with him. It is God who saves. If your friend rejects the gospel, it is not you he is rejecting.

The apostle Paul reminds us of this important fact in 1 Corinthians 3:6, "I planted the seed, Apollos watered it, but God made it grow."

Keep planting and watering the gospel seed with both your life and your lips and watch God work. Your continued friendship might be what God uses to ultimately draw your friend to salvation.

Let the following outline of John 3:16 serve as a tool for you as you seek to hold the rope and get your friends close to Jesus. Why John 3:16? Because it is the most quoted verse in all the Bible, and it summarizes God's plan for man in 4 summary statements. These summary statements clearly outline what one must hear in order to receive the greatest gift possible.

The proclamation of the gospel is powerful and necessary for getting people close to Jesus! In Romans 1:16 Paul declares, "I am not ashamed of the gospel, for it is the power of God for the salvation of everyone who believes…"

There is power in the gospel and John 3:16 is a great verse to explain it clearly and effectively. Learn it, share it, and watch God use you to become a change agent in your circle of influence.

"For God so loved the world that he gave his one and only Son, that whoever believes in him shall not perish but have eternal life." (John 3:16).

Before, I present this method to you, let me caution you to not try to memorize the following paragraphs word for word. They are simply meant to be a guide for you. Read them several times to familiarize yourself with the Truth contained in them, and the order they are presented. The more comfortable you become, the more confidence you will gain. As you grow in your confidence, you will be more likely to engage in spiritual conversations. It will be in these spiritual conversations where doors will open for you to share the gospel with your friends. Now, pray for God to guide you and have fun as you learn another tool to help you hold the rope and get your friends close to Jesus.

The first summary statement is God's plan. His plan is to love the world. Notice the beginning of the verse, "For God so loved the world." Here the writer tells that God's ultimate plan is to have a love relationship with all of mankind. He desires to love you and for you to love Him. God is not so interested in religion; rather, He is interested in a relationship. More than anything else, because of His great love for you, God desires to relate to you in a very real and personal way.

God did not create man out of need; rather, He created man out of desire. God desired fellowship with the highest of all His creation. However, many are not experiencing this love relationship with God because they have a problem.

The second summary statement clearly defines this problem. Man's problem is sin. The word "perish" in the verse indicates that man truly has this sin problem. What is sin? Many think sin is when a person breaks one of the Ten Commandments like, "Thou shall not steal." While this is true, sin is so much more than just breaking one of the Ten

Commandments. There are 3 words in the Hebrew language that define sin. These words together teach sin is anything that offends God. This is to include man's thoughts, his actions, and anything else man fails to do to please God.

The Bible makes it very clear all have sinned. No one is perfect, not even you, and especially not me. The Bible also makes it clear that sin causes separation from God, and if a person dies physically separated from God, he will spend forever in a real place called hell. This is bad news. Fortunately for all, the verse does not end with this summary statement. There is good news! Keep reading, and you will discover it.

The good news is found in the third summary statement, God's remedy. While man has a problem, God has a remedy. Look back in the verse as it reads, "He gave his one and only Son."

God's remedy for sin is Jesus. God sent His one and only Son to earth by way of a virgin named Mary who was supernaturally conceived by the Holy Spirit. Jesus, being God in the flesh, was tempted in all ways, yet He lived without sin. He lived an absolutely perfect life. He never offended the Father in heaven.

After living this perfect life, Jesus died a sacrificial death on a cruel cross. He was then buried in a borrowed tomb just as the Bible predicted would happen. On the third day, Jesus was supernaturally raised from the dead, defeating death, hell and the grave. He lived the life man could not, died a death man deserved, and was raised from the dead to give the gift of eternal life man could not earn.

However, it is not enough to just know these important facts. While God has a remedy for man's problem, man still has to respond. The fourth and final summary statement, man's response, is found in the following, "that whoever believes in him."

Man has to respond to the facts as God draws him. Salvation is more than mere head knowledge, it is from the heart. When man fully understands who Jesus is, and what He did he must respond by believing in Him. This word "believe" described in this verse is not simply accepting that the facts discussed are true. It is a complete surrendering to the person Jesus Christ.

There is a story told of the amazing Charles Blondin, a famous French tightrope walker who crossed Niagara Falls. This story can be used to illustrate what it really means to believe.

It is believed that in June of 1859, Blondin became the first person to cross a tightrope stretched over a quarter of a mile across the mighty Niagara Falls. He walked across 160 feet above the falls a few different times, each time with a different daring feat – once solo, once with an empty wheelbarrow, and then again with a wheelbarrow filled with sand!

After safely pushing across the wheelbarrow filled with sand, Blondin asked the crowd if they believed he could push the wheelbarrow safely across with a man inside of it. The large crowd that had gathered "ooohed" and "aaaahed" with excitement and anticipation. They all shouted in unison, "Yes, we believe!"

Blondin then asked the question that brought a hush over the crowd, "Who will volunteer to get in the wheelbarrow?"

As you may have guessed, at first, no one volunteered. Surely the onlookers knew it was possible for him to do this amazing feat, yet no one was willing put their life in Blondin's hands. Therefore, in its truest sense, no one really believed. For believing is more than just giving an intellectual assent, true belief is a matter of the heart and demands a response.

As the story continues to unfold, a young man in the back of the crowd shouted out that he would be willing to get into the wheelbarrow. Blondin then very carefully and cautiously pushed the young man safely across the falls and then back again. The crowd cheered so loudly their applause was louder than the roar of the falls!

The young man believed not just with his head; he believed with his whole heart as was demonstrated in his response to put his life in Blondin's hands. This story, whether it is factual or fictional, paints a real life picture of what faith actually is.

Faith is when you relinquish full control of your life to the person of Jesus Christ believing He alone has the power to free you from your sin. Faith is when you are comfortable to step out not knowing fully what the day holds because you are confident you know fully the One who holds the day.

The four summary statements are simple and very effective. They open up the central Truth found in the

Bible and can be shared anywhere. Below are a couple of examples of how simple it is to put the above information into practice.

I was at a leadership conference at First Baptist Woodstock years ago. During one of the breaks, my friend and I left to eat in a local restaurant by the church. Many of the other ministers who were at the conference also had the same idea and beat us to the restaurant. When my friend and I were greeted by the hostess, we were given a choice to wait about 30 minutes for a seat or to be seated at the bar. I noticed a man sitting at the bar drinking a beer and quickly requested to be seated next to him.

Once we were seated, we placed our orders, and then I began to make small talk with the man at the bar. After learning a little about him, I asked him if he ever read his Bible. He confessed reading the Bible was not his normal practice although he owned one. I then asked him what he thought the most quoted verse of all times was. To my surprise, he answered with John 3:16. I then asked him if he had an opinion of why it was the most quoted verse. He did not and asked me if I did. I told him I did and asked him if I could show him on a napkin. I then wrote down all 4 summary statements carefully explaining each one of them just like I did for you earlier in this chapter. Before I finished my lunch that day, the man bowed his head at the bar and invited Jesus Christ to be his Lord and Savior. I then took his contact information and gave it to the outreach pastor of the church.

I was so excited that the very next day during our lunch break from the conference, my friend and I went to another restaurant and requested to be seated at the bar. We were seated next to 5 construction workers. They were already enjoying their burgers, chicken wings and beer. I began asking them questions about their work and their lives. They were each eager to share. Eventually they would ask me some questions, and I shared with them a little about my life as well.

I asked if any of them enjoyed reading their Bible. They all confessed that Bible reading was not a habit for them.

I asked if any of them had an idea what the most quoted verse in all of the Bible was. They all responded with a no.

Then, I asked them if they had ever noticed the guy in the end zone who held up the poster board with the letters JN and the numbers 3:16 on it. They all agreed they had seen a guy holding this type of a sign at a game.

I asked them if they had a clue what the letters and numbers meant. They did not have a clue.

I shared with them it was a Bible verse, and it represented the most quoted verse of all time. They were interested and actually asked me why it was so popular. I then pulled out a napkin, wrote down the verse, and walked them through the four summary statements I shared with you earlier in this chapter. They all listened as they ate.

After clearly presenting the summary statements to them, I asked if any of them had ever truly believed in the Lord Jesus Christ. They all replied negatively. The men and I continued to talk as we ate. They seemed to genuinely enjoy our conversation. And to my surprise, as my friend and I went to pay our bill, one of the construction workers had anonymously already taken care of our check.

Since the meetings at the 2 bars in Woodstock, Georgia, I have had the opportunity to share John 3:16 in many different places. There have been times like at the first bar where individuals responded positively to the gospel and surrendered their lives to Christ, and there have been many times like at the second bar where individuals listened but rejected the gospel. Whether the individuals accepted Christ or rejected Him, I was 100% successful with the call God has placed on my life. While it is our responsibility to hold the rope and get people close to Jesus, ultimately only God can draw a sinner to repentance. We cannot save our friends, but if we get them close enough to Jesus, God sure can!

CHAPTER 10

HOLD THE ROPE THROUGH PRAYER

Prayer is the fuel for life and evangelism. However, many take prayer for granted. Too many people are like the pastor I once heard about who called in sick one Sunday to go bear hunting. After a long day in the woods with no bear sightings, the pastor decided to give up. On his way back to his vehicle, he heard the loud roar of a bear. Making his way to the noise, the pastor tripped and fell down a nine foot embankment.

The bear heard the noise from the pastor's fall and went to investigate. The pastor realized he had dropped his rifle and that there was a bear approaching him. The pastor got up and took off as fast as he could; however, the bear was gaining ground.

The pastor made the mistake of looking back as he was running away. He hit a stump with his foot and fell to the ground. As the bear was almost on top of him, the pastor shouted out a prayer in desperation, "O God of heaven, please make this bear a Christian."

The bear stopped dead in his tracks, got down on his knees, put his paws together, bowed his head and said, "Dear God, please bless this man I am about to eat."

The pastor used prayer as a last resort just like we do sometimes. Prayer was not meant to be our last resort. It was meant to be our first response. Jesus is not our spare tire, nor is He our copilot. He is the Master of our lives and as fully devoted followers of Christ, we should imitate Him and start our day with prayer.

"Very early in the morning, while it was still dark, Jesus got up, left the house and went off to a solitary place, where he prayed." (Mark 1:35).

Jesus started His day with prayer, and we should too. Think about it for a moment. If the Son of God on earth believed it to be necessary to spend time with His Father in heaven each morning through prayer, how much more do you and I need to start each day with prayer? Prayer at the beginning of the day will help us become more aware of God's presence in our lives and position us to draw from His power. And we need this power for living and for holding the rope!

Our prayer life should consist of adoration and thanksgiving. We should praise God for who He is and thank Him for all He has done. God is unbelievably good to us. He gives us what we do not deserve, and He does not give us what we do deserve. His grace and mercy flow freely to us through faith in Christ. He is holy and awesome. We should praise and thank Him each day as we rise up, and according to the apostle Paul, we should praise and thank Him throughout the day as well.

"Be joyful always; pray continually; give thanks in all circumstances, for this is God's will for you in Christ Jesus." (1 Thessalonians 5:16-18).

Praise and thanksgiving should come as natural to us as breathing. They should regularly flow from our lips. Confession should be a regular part of our prayer life. Jesus taught us this in his great sermon on the mountain, "Forgive us our debts, as we also have forgiven our debtors." (Matthew 6:12).

When we humbly go before the Lord daily in confession, He frees us from the guilt of our sin and gives us the power we need to forgive others and to live for Him. (1 John 1:9). Please do not think for one minute we do not have anything to confess. Yes, in Christ, we are positionally perfect; however, practically speaking, you and I fall short every day. We need to regularly bring our prayers of confession to the Lord.

Our prayers should be filled with both the passions and the people God has placed on our hearts. Concerning our passions, he tells us, "Ask and it will be given to you; seek and you will find; knock and the door will be opened to you. For everyone who asks receives; he who seeks finds; and to him who knocks, the door will be opened." (Matthew 7:7-8). Concerning people, we will always benefit from talking with God about people before we talk with them about God. Let me illustrate this truth with the following testimony of one of our senior team members.

Siolo Tauaefa grew up on the streets of Hawaii. From a very early age, he got involved with drugs, alcohol, and gang activity. It is safe to say his teenage years were filled with chaos and confusion. However, God would bring into his life a beautiful, young Christian lady who would sweep him off of his feet.

Siolo got married and starting attending church periodically with his new bride. Although he wasn't involved in gang activity anymore, he still did not totally surrender to Christ. He pretty much just went to church to pacify his wife. His wife, Chloe, was involved in a young couples home Bible study and regularly asked him to attend with her. However, Siolo always came up with a good excuse of why he could not attend. This did not deter Chloe and her home Bible study group from praying for Siolo's salvation. The more he would make excuses, the more they would pray.

One night, the group was meeting for Bible study, but Siolo headed to the gym for the regularly scheduled pick up basketball game instead. Siolo left early because the gym was always packed, and he wanted to get on a good team. However, when he arrived at the gym, the manager was the only one there. Siolo went in, shot around for 20 minutes or so, and then asked the manager if the games had been cancelled. The manager informed him nothing had been cancelled and did not understand why the other guys had not shown up. Siolo waited a little while longer and then headed home.

On his way home, he stopped at an intersection and found himself contemplating whether he should turn one way for his home or another way for the Bible study. He testifies regularly how God prompted him to turn toward the Bible study. He soon arrived, and as he opened the door to the home, they were all praying together for his salvation. That night Siolo confessed his sin and believed on the Lord Jesus Christ for his salvation.

Today Siolo has an incredible family who loves him very much. He is on the leadership board of Team Impact. He no longer lives in the chaos and confusion that once characterized his life. He walks with the peace of Jesus in his heart and has one of the most infectious smiles ever. Siolo's eternal destination has been changed from hell to heaven, and his wife and her home Bible study group's prayers played a major role in getting him close to Jesus.

Because this principle of praying for the lost is so important, I have included some Scriptures designed to help us as we pray for our friends and family who are far from God.

We must pray that:

God draws them to Himself.
John 6:44

They seek to know God.
Acts 17:27

Satan is bound from blinding them to the truth.
2 Corinthians 4:4

Strongholds will be demolished.
2 Corinthians 10:3-4

The Holy Spirit works in them.
John 16:8-11

They believe the Scriptures.
1 Thessalonians 2:13

God grants them repentance.
2 Timothy 2:24-26

They turn from sin.
Acts 17:30-31

They believe in Christ as Savior.
John 1:12

They confess Christ as Lord.
Romans 10:9-10

They yield all to follow Christ.
2 Corinthians 5:15

As we pray for our friends who are far from the Lord, we must ask God for boldness. We must ask Him to fill us with the courage necessary to step out in faith and hold the rope. Holding the rope can at times be frightening and frustrating. Boldness will enable us to take risks and to do whatever is necessary to hold the rope and get our friends close to Jesus. We must be willing to do anything to hold the rope as long as it is not illegal, immoral, or unethical. Boldness will give us this crazy courage. As we pray for boldness, let us not forget, "For God did not give us a spirit of timidity, but a spirit of power, of love, and of self- discipline." (2 Timothy 1:7-8).

While in prayer, we must also ask the Lord to raise up others to join us in this rope holding effort. In Matthew 9:37-38, Jesus said, "The harvest is plentiful, but the workers are few. Ask the Lord of the harvest, therefore, to send out workers into his harvest field."

As an old business friend of mine once said, "It takes a team to build the dream." We must pray for others to develop a passion for the lost. We must ask God to raise up men, women, boys and girls who possess a great burden for those who are dead in their sins.

Years ago in seminary, I remember reading in a leading evangelical magazine that only 1 out of every 10 Christians share their faith. Only prayer will change this statistic. Pray regularly for God to raise up likeminded people who will do whatever it takes to hold the rope and get others close to Jesus.

We must ask God for a deep compassion for the lost. We must ask Him to burn deep within our hearts a real desire to see those in our circle of influence come to faith in Christ. The apostle Paul wrote in Romans 10:1, "Brothers, my heart's desire and prayer to God … is that they may be saved." We know this compassion moved Paul to dedicate his life to holding the rope for those in his day. We must ask for this same compassion to move us out of our comfortable routines and into the risky relationships with those who are far from God. Heaven and hell hang in the balance. Many of those in our circle of influence are counting on us to hold the rope so they can get close to Jesus.

Prayer truly does make a difference. God hears our prayers, and He really answers them. When we pray, we touch the very heart of God, and He responds for our benefit. If you struggle with this truth, take a moment and read 2 Kings 20:1-7. Notice how the events of this passage unfold. The prophet Amoz tells King Hezekiah he should set his house in order because he is going to die. The king prays earnestly to God for his life. The Bible clearly states God heard the king's cry and added 15 years to his life. I cannot tell you how our prayers for the lost will move God, but I can tell you He wants to hear from us. He wants to work in and through us to reach our friends with the gospel.

Prayer unlocks the power of the Holy Spirit within us and enables us to hold the rope and get our friends close to Jesus. Talking with and listening to God is key in living for

God and holding the rope for our friends. Remember, he who has prayed well, has prepared well

CHAPTER 11

WAKE UP AND
HOLD THE ROPE

Though only in the fifth grade, young Toby knew how to share about the truth contained in God's Word. Toby was recounting the story of Jonah and the great fish to some of his friends when he was overheard by his atheist teacher.

In a voice loud enough for all the class to hear, the teacher said, "You don't really believe Jonah was actually swallowed by a real fish do you?"

With a quick nod of his head, Toby replied, "I sure do."

The teacher proclaimed, "Impossible, it cannot be true!"

"I do not know how it happened, but my Bible says it did so I believe it." He grew more boldly with every word.

"In fact, when I get to heaven one day I will ask Jonah just how it happened."

With a smirk on his face, the teacher sighed loudly and said, "What if Jonah is not in Heaven when you get there?"

"Well then you can ask him."

Usually with the story of Jonah, we focus on him being consumed by a large fish and then being coughed up on dry land. However, if we take a closer look, in Jonah 1:1-10, there is much more to the story.

The word of the LORD came to Jonah son of Amittai: "Go to the great city of Nineveh and preach against it, because its wickedness has come up before me."

But Jonah ran away from the LORD and headed for Tarshish. He went down to Joppa, where he found a ship bound for that port. After paying the fare, he went aboard and sailed for Tarshish to flee from the LORD.

Then the LORD sent a great wind on the sea, and such a violent storm arose that the ship threatened to break up. All the sailors were afraid and each cried out to his own god. And they threw the cargo into the sea to lighten the ship.

But Jonah had gone below deck, where he lay down and fell into a deep sleep. The captain went to him and said, "How can you sleep? Get up and call on your god! Maybe he will take notice of us, and we will not perish."

Then the sailors said to each other, "Come, let us cast lots to find out who is responsible for this calamity." They cast lots, and the lot fell on Jonah.

So they asked him, "Tell us, who is responsible for making all this trouble for us? What do you do? Where do you come from? What is your country? From what people are you?"

He answered, "I am a Hebrew, and I worship the LORD, the God of heaven, who made the sea and the land."

This terrified them, and they asked, "What have you done?" (They knew he was running away from the LORD, because he had already told them so.)

Envision what you have just read. Jonah is told to go by God to preach in Ninevah. However, rather than be obedient, he decides to go to Tarshish.

Are you Jonah? Has God asked you to witness to someone, but instead, you decided to do your own thing? God's ultimate plan, however, is going to be fulfilled as the story continues.

As Jonah shares the truth, he explains that his God has caused the storm, and his God can stop it. The next question from the sailors to Jonah is particularly poignant, "What is this you have done?" (Jonah 1:10).

Those being thrown about by the storm do not understand how Jonah could sleep contently on the bottom of the boat while they were about to lose their lives. How could Jonah sleep with the answer?

Though not physically asleep, I believe a great number of the church is spiritually asleep while those around them are being tormented by the world and going to hell. The church needs to wake up. Are you consciously choosing to hold the rope and share the love of Jesus? Or, are you asleep in the bottom of the boat?

A couple of months ago, I was in the gym when a man I barely knew started to talk to me. I had seen this man in the gym for several years. From previous conversations, I knew he attended church. He began to tell me a story about one of his co- workers who had a son who was afflicted with cancer. He was wrestling with how God's sovereignty could allow a twelve year old boy to be so very sick.

A couple of years ago, this young boy had been out in the front yard playing football when he came in the house complaining of a headache. This simple headache turned out to be a cancerous brain tumor. Over the last couple of years, the cancer had gone into remission, but now it had started spreading rapidly over his entire body. The young boy was given two weeks to live. At work, they decided to donate money to send the boy and his family to Disney World. The trip had to be cut short because the young boy started to take a turn for the worse.

As this gentleman and I began to wonder what God's purpose in all this might be, I finally asked him the question I had been holding back. I asked, "Hey brother, have you gotten the chance to witness to this family about the love of Jesus through this whole process?"

After a 5 second pause, he stammered, "No I just think that is kinda personal, and I don't want to offend them."

I was stunned. I couldn't believe his response. His co-worker was in turmoil, and his family was in complete upheaval. The storms of life were shaking up his friends' lives, and he was completely silent about the only thing that could bring his friend lasting peace. How could he "sleep in the bottom of the boat" while his co-worker and his entire family were being destroyed? An unbelieving world cannot fathom how we could have the answer and not share it with them.

There is an obvious dissonance that is communicated to the world when we say there is a real place called hell, and yet we do not care enough to tell them truth about Christ. How can we sleep with the knowledge that many in the world today will face an eternity separated from a Holy God?

Jesus said it this way in John 4:34-38:

> "My food is to do the will of him who sent me and to finish his work. Do you not say, 'Four months more and then the harvest'? I tell you, open your eyes and look at the fields! They are ripe for harvest. Even now the reaper draws his wages, even now he harvests the crop for eternal life, so that the sower and the reaper may be glad together. Thus the saying 'One sows and another reaps' is true. I sent you to reap what you have not worked for. Others have done the hard work, and you have reaped the benefits of their labor."

"Four months more and then the harvest" was a proverb that basically means you cannot rush the harvest.

Jesus contradicts this and says there are lost people, right now, who need to hear about Jesus. Will you wake up and join God in His great and sovereign plan of redemption? God wants to use you.

My six year old son Graham loves to help me clean the garage. Of course, I allow him to assist me in the job. However, my motivation in allowing him to help me is not that the job gets done faster. In fact, it usually takes twice as long. We take everything out of the garage. Of course, he wants to help me lift every heavy item. Finally, we get our brooms out and begin to sweep all of the debris onto the driveway. After it is completely cleaned, we return all of the items back to their proper place, and we proudly look upon a job well done.

Graham's face will have a half-smile with sharp dimples that lets me know that the work was worth it to him. For the next few days, when we walk into the garage, he will tell me, "Daddy, remember when we rolled the bikes out and cleaned that corner?" The reason why I let him help me was not because the job was easier with him. No, I let him help me because it changes him.

The sovereign God of the universe could save sinful men in any manner He chose. However, in His infinite wisdom, He has chosen to enlist you and me in His marvelous plan of redemption. When you and I are engaged in this process, people get saved. But just as important, God allows us to partner with Him because it changes us.

If you are asleep in the bottom of the boat, this is a challenge to wake up. The omniscient God of the universe wants you to join Him as he redeems sinful men. Not because you have the power to redeem them, but because you know the One who does.

CONCLUSION

By now it should be crystal clear. God is calling you to hold the rope and get your friends close to Jesus. It is time for you to spread your wings of evangelism and fly. People are hanging in the balance. Souls are at stake. Your voice can make an eternal difference in the lives of the lost. Your voice may serve as the gap between heaven and hell for someone.

As the call has been made loudly and clearly, so should your voice ring. Silence is no longer an option. It is time for you to get filled up and fired up. Then you must stand up and speak up for the cause of Christ. You must go until Jesus comes, and you must share until all have heard of his incredible sacrifice. You must do all you can to hold the rope and get people close to Jesus.

Before you wake up tomorrow, the destiny of thousands of people will be forever changed. Sobering research reveals that in a typical day in the United States:

- More than 10,000 people will be born while more than 6,000 people will die.

- Almost 100 suicides will take place.
- More than 40 people will die from alcohol- related vehicle accidents.
- Simultaneously there will be more than 6,000 marriages and 3,000 divorces.
- More than 3,000 unmarried women will give birth to a child while more than 3,000 abortions will take place.
- More than 40 people with the AIDS virus will die.
- Almost 5,000 fifteen-year-old girls will have sexual intercourse for the first time.
- More than 1,300 students will drop out of high school giving up on their dreams.
- Almost 30,000 people will be arrested.
- Almost 5,000 drug related violations will take place.
- Over 60,000 people will receive food stamps.

In that same 24-hour period, thousands of people will reach a turning point in their spiritual lives:

- 6 new Christian churches in the United States will open their doors for the first time while 8 will close their doors for the last time.
- Over 400 people will convert to Islam
- Over 800 people will become Mormons
- Most importantly, in the United States, over the next 24 hours, thousands of people will die without knowing Jesus Christ personally and spend forever separated from God in a real place called hell.

While the above statistics are both startling and sobering, let them exhort you to hear the cry of the lost. They are crying out in their own way, like the Philippian jailer, "Sirs what must I do to be saved." (Acts 16:30).

We will be praying for you as you step out in faith, hold the rope, and get your friends close to Jesus!

ABOUT THE AUTHORS

Jeff Neal

Jeff graduated from Howard Payne University. He then played six years of professional football where he earned the title as one of the NFL's strongest men and the nickname, the "Man of Steel." His extraordinary strength earned him several national and world power lifting titles.

Jeff considers all of his accolades a loss compared to the surpassing greatness of knowing Jesus Christ as Lord and Savior. He is eminently concerned with winning the lost and acutely sensitive to the needs of others.

Jeff's desire to reach the world with the gospel and his extraordinary strength led him to partner with a group of close friends to start the ministry of Team Impact in 2000.

Jeff's leadership on the Team Impact board has contributed to the preaching of the gospel to millions of people around the globe and to hundreds of thousands of salvations. Jeff grew up in Houston, Texas and now resides in Corinth, Texas with his wife Cindy and their three children Brooke, Dawson and Graham.

Shonn Keels

Shonn graduated from the University of South Carolina and Luther Rice Seminary. He married Bonnie Powell on May 22, 1993. He and his wife have two girls, Brelin and Baylee. They currently reside in Myrtle Beach, South Carolina. Shonn has been a long-time student of leadership and evangelism, working diligently to develop these gifts and to challenge others to do the same.

Shonn has a vision for the world. He has worked to provide evangelism and leadership training resources to church leaders in the United States, Brazil, Zambia, the Ukraine, Australia, South Africa and India.

Shonn's travels have taken him to more than 30 countries, almost all of the States in the U.S. and to 6 of the 7 continents. He has spoken face to face with more than 1 million people in his ministry and has witnessed tens of thousands of people make decisions for the Lord Jesus Christ. His passion for evangelism is evident and contagious.

Shonn is the cofounder of the Carolina Forest Community Center. The community center is shaping the future of Horry County by providing recreational programs that develop competence and character and help build stronger families and positive relationships in a Christ-centered atmosphere. The community center is influencing several thousand people annually. Shonn is the former senior pastor of Carolina Forest Community Church and is the President of Shonn Keels Ministries, Inc. He and his family spend much time on the road encouraging pastors and their congregations to maximize their redemptive potential.

Shonn is no stranger to the gym. He has always believed the disciplines learned in the weight room are transferable to life. His tenacity in the gym and his desire to reach people have earned him a spot on the internationally known strongmen for Christ, Team Impact. He has been traveling the world since 1997 doing feats of strength and sharing the gospel with this generation.

Shonn is also the author of Maximize Your Leadership. You can keep up with Shonn and order his materials at www.shonnkeels.com.

TEAM IMPACT
MINISTRY